Breaking the *Good Girl* Syndrome

How Freedom Repaired What Religion Damaged

TIFFANY MELVIN

Breaking the Good Girl Syndrome:
How Freedom Repaired What Religion Damaged
Tiffany Sherrell Melvin, The Freedom Frame™,
Creative Council Studios™, Copyright © 2025

EMPOWER ME BOOKS, INC.
A Subsidiary of Empower Me Enterprises, Inc.
https://www.empowermeenterprises.com

No part of this book may be reproduced, stored in a retrieval system, or transmitted in any form or by electronic, mechanical, photocopying, recording, scanning, or otherwise, without the publisher's prior written permission.

The names and identifying characteristics of certain individuals and places referenced in this publication have been changed.

The author extends the courtesy that this publication should not be viewed as an antagonist against the Faith, but rather as a contender of the Faith and an advocate of a relationship with our Lord Jesus Christ. This publication is a promoter of Shepards After the Heart of the Father of our Lord and Savior Jesus Christ. This publication contains the thoughts, opinions, and ideas of its author.

Scripture Permissions

Scripture quotations marked (NIV) are taken from the Holy Bible, New International Version®, NIV®. Copyright © 1973, 1978, 1984, 2011 by Biblica, Inc.™ Used by permission. All rights reserved worldwide.

Scripture quotations marked (KJV) are from the King James Version of the Bible. Public domain.

Scripture quotations marked (NKJV) are from the New King James Version®. Copyright © 1982 by Thomas Nelson. Used by permission. All rights reserved.

Scripture quotations marked (NLT) are from the Holy Bible, New Living Translation®, Copyright © 1996, 2004, 2015 by Tyndale House Foundation. Used by permission of Tyndale House Publishers, Inc., Carol Stream, Illinois 60188. All rights reserved.

Scripture quotations marked (MSG) are from *The Message*. Copyright © 1993–2002 by Eugene H. Peterson. Used by permission of NavPress. All rights reserved.

Scripture quotations marked (CSB) are from the Christian Standard Bible®, Copyright © 2017 by Holman Bible Publishers. Used by permission. Christian Standard Bible® and CSB® are federally registered trademarks of Holman Bible Publishers.

Scripture quotations marked (ESV) are from *The Holy Bible, English Standard Version® (ESV)*. Copyright © 2001 by Crossway, a publishing ministry of Good News Publishers. Used by permission. All rights reserved.

ISBN: 978-1954418509
Printed in the United States of America

First Edition: October 31, 2025

Breaking the *Good Girl* Syndrome

How Freedom Repaired What Religion Damaged

DEDICATIONS

I dedicate this book to every WOMAN who will say yes to their healing and be compelled to freedom because of my story. As an ambassador of Christ, I decree peace, love, strength and joy over you now, in Jesus' name!

To my maternal grandmother, Hattie Pearl Dunston-Alston,
Thank you for showing me that good things like love, strength, dedication, dignity, and honor can indeed come in small packages. I will never forget you for showing me at an early age what true love for family really looks like. I will forever love you — your granddaughter, Sherrell, as you so lovingly called me!

To my Aunt Lillie Beatrice Alston-King, who was like a second mother to me:
You are the one who taught me how important it was to have Jesus in my life. There was so much I wanted to share with you about my freedom journey, but I never got the chance to. During your transition, God allowed me to hear you pleading for your family, which is indicative of who I knew you to be. So please know that the very thing you pleaded for — I GOT IT! Thank you for loving me, and I am so glad that on January 23, 2023, you got a chance to step into the room with truth and freedom to take your rest. **YOU ARE FREE!** I dedicate my journey of freedom to you. RIP — I love you dearly!

CONTENTS

Foreword: **Apostle, Dr. Dawn R. Smith**

Introduction: When Religion Wounds and Freedom Heals
Freedom in Christ is not rebellion—it is restoration

PART I: THE MAKING OF A GOOD GIRL
How Religion Crafted a Mask I Couldn't Breathe Through

Chapter 1 – Fear in a Dress: My Childhood in Religion

Theme: Legalism disguised as holiness
Focus: Holiness culture, early prophetic experiences, fear-based faith
Takeaway: Fear is not the language of God—love is

Chapter 2 – When Tears Were My Voice

Theme: Emotion as a prophetic language
Focus: Emotional sensitivity, shame, family pain, and identity suppression
Takeaway: Tears are valid. Sensitivity is a gift, not a weakness

Chapter 3 – Raised by Rules, Not Relationship

Theme: Transaction over intimacy
Focus: Legalism, shame-based theology, and the poverty mindset
Takeaway: Relationship with God begins where performance ends

CONTENTS

INSTRUCTOR PLANNING SECTION:

CONTENTS

PART II: The Collapse of Control
What Happens When You Realize Religion Isn't Healing You

Chapter 4 – The High Cost of Trying to Be Good

Theme: The breaking point
Focus: Family betrayal, identity shrinking, performance-based guilt
Takeaway: When goodness costs you your voice and freedom, it's not from God

Chapter 5 – Deliverance or Disguise?

Theme: The illusion of spiritual safety
Focus: Spiritual manipulation, abusive marriage, and failed rededications
Takeaway: Deliverance that comes from control is not freedom—it's bondage

Chapter 6 – Leaving Church, Not Christ

Theme: Unlearning religion, rediscovering God
Focus: Absence from church, inner torment, understanding salvation
Takeaway: Your salvation is not tied to a building—it's anchored in relationship

CONTENTS

INSTRUCTOR PLANNING SECTION:

CONTENTS

PART III: THE DIVINE INTERRUPTION
When God Rescues You from the Very Thing That Claimed to Represent Him

Chapter 7 – The Epiphany That Broke the Chains

Theme: Rhema revelation and deprogramming
Focus: God's correction as love, breaking religious fear, freedom through repentance
Takeaway: True deliverance begins with asking for the truth—no matter how painful

Chapter 8 – When the Wilderness Is the Rescue

Theme: Isolation as a sanctuary
Focus: Spiritual burnout, accidents, quiet healing, Breath of Life experience
Takeaway: The wilderness isn't abandonment—it's divine rescue

Chapter 9 – Diagnosing the Root, Not the Fruit

Theme: Heart work over behavior modification
Focus: Boundary-setting, truth-telling, and emotional honesty
Takeaway: God heals the root—not just the symptoms

CONTENTS

INSTRUCTOR PLANNING SECTION:

CONTENTS

PART IV: THE BECOMING
Stepping into the Identity I Was Always Meant to Carry

Chapter 10 – Unshackled but Still Shaped

Theme: Lingering effects of religious trauma
Focus: Rebuilding voice, boldness, fear of backlash
Takeaway: Freedom requires practice, not just permission

Chapter 11 – Finding My True Voice

Theme: Identity in Christ
Focus: Boldness, God-confidence, prophetic clarity
Takeaway: God doesn't need you to be perfect—just authentic

Chapter 12 – A New Kind of Holiness

Theme: Redefining purity
Focus: Holiness rooted in intimacy, not external standards
Takeaway: True holiness is relational, not performative

CONTENTS

INSTRUCTOR PLANNING SECTION:

CONTENTS

PART V: THE FREEDOM COMMISSION
An Invitation to Everyone Ready to Come Out

Chapter 13 – Freedom is a Person

Theme:	Jesus-centered deliverance
Focus:	Walking with the Holy Spirit, resting in grace
Takeaway:	Freedom isn't an event—it's a relationship

Chapter 14 – Repaired, Reclaimed, and Recommissioned

Theme:	Apostolic restoration
Focus:	Returning to calling, legacy, and Kingdom authority
Takeaway:	God repairs what religion damaged—so you can lead others to freedom

AFTERWORD: APOSTLE SHAY JOHNSON

ACKNOWLEDGEMENTS
ABOUT the AUTHOR
CALL to ACTION
BOOK REVIEWS

CONTENTS

INSTRUCTOR PLANNING SECTION:

FOREWORD

— BY DR. DAWN R. SMITH —

The "Good Girl Syndrome" is more than a behavior—it is a stronghold. For many, it begins in childhood, born from trauma or bloodline iniquities. It shapes how we see ourselves and silently conditions how we respond to the world. Over time, these false versions of ourselves harden into false identities, and we learn to live behind masks we cannot breathe through.

But our true identity is not formed in fear, shame, or performance. Our true identity originates with our Heavenly Father, who holds the original blueprint of who He created us to be. Just as an earthly father is called to provide security, protection, and identity, so our Heavenly Father longs to do the same. Yet, for so many, this truth is hidden or untaught.

We end up searching for belonging and worth in things never meant to define us—systems, people, and even religion. The result is bondage that may look like goodness on the outside but feels like suffocation on the inside.

This is why Tiffany Melvin's Breaking the Good Girl Syndrome is such a vital, Holy Spirit–breathed work. Tiffany takes us on a journey that mirrors the process of deliverance itself: exposure, collapse, and restoration. Through the details of her story, she gives us both a picture and a reference point to connect with.

Her eye for detail draws us into her life's narrative and reveals how God transformed her from the inside out.

It was within this same journey of healing that I met Tiffany. We were first introduced in July 2021 at a conference in Raleigh, NC. Our meeting was brief, facilitated by a mutual friend. Our paths crossed again in October 2022 at another Raleigh conference where I was vending. In hindsight, even the names of those gatherings—Mantled for Miracles and Dwell: A Gathering of Warriors, Intercessors, and Watchmen—tell a prophetic story of healing.

This second encounter gave us the opportunity to talk more deeply. What first drew Tiffany was the fragrance emanating from my table. As I shared my journey in ministry, a bond was born. Since then, I have had the privilege of witnessing Tiffany's healing journey unfold, watching her go from glory to glory. What I admire most is her willingness to pursue the promises of God, trusting that His answer is always "yes and amen." Even when facing fear, she presses through with the guidance of the Holy Spirit. Tiffany is living proof that Jehovah Shammah—the Lord is there—is indeed with us.

Tiffany's words carry both prophetic clarity and compassion. She writes as one who has walked through the fire and emerged free. She dismantles the illusion that performance can please God and instead calls us to true freedom—intimacy with Christ. In her voice, holiness is no longer a mask but a relationship, and freedom is not rebellion but restoration.

As you read, may your heart awaken to the Father's voice, calling you out of the "good girl" identity and into your authentic, God-given design. May you trade striving for rest, rules for relationship, and fear for the perfect love that casts it out. And may you, like Tiffany, discover that the One who breaks chains still restores, recommissions, and calls His daughters into freedom in Him.

— Apostle Dr. Dawn R. Smith
Founder, The Esther Experience ®
Owner, Restoring Balance Holistic ®
Raleigh, NC

INTRODUCTION

When Religion Wounds and Freedom Heals

I can't really recall a time in my life when I didn't feel bound or fearful of something. Whether it was fear of people's opinions, fear of embarrassment, fear of not being liked, fear of making the wrong decision, fear of judgment, fear of the unknown, fear of dying and going to hell, fear of the enemy, fear of God's punishment, self-condemnation, shame, guilt, overthinking, perfectionism, anxiety—you name it, and it seems like I feared it.

There was so much fear that all my life I felt heavy. Even when I walked around giddy, full of laughter, and seemed not to have a care in the world, I never felt free. **BUT GOD**!

In 2018, the Most High God came to cause a divine interruption in my life to bring me to a place of freedom in Him. I received that prophetic rhema word on April 15, 2018—the day I stepped into Breath of Life Church[1] on a cane, full of heartache, heartbreak, physical pain, mental anguish, disappointment, fear, anger, and depression.

---

[1] The Church Name has been changed to protect the integrity of the work of the Lord that is being completed through the vessels that serve as the Founders of this Faith-based Institution.

God told me He had purposed this spiritual transition for my freedom. I won't say I had a full understanding of what He was saying to me then, but I was in so much agony, I was just grateful to hear from God—because religion had told me He was mad at me for some reason and was punishing me.

Through this healing and freedom journey, I've learned so much about God and myself, and I now know those previous thoughts about Him were so far from the truth.

By now, I'm guessing you've read the foreword and all the good ole dedications that come with writing a book—or maybe you're like me and skipped all that to get to this hot and juicy story of *"How Freedom Repaired What Religion Damaged."*

Maybe you are someone who also feels as though you've been bound and/or damaged by religion but have been afraid to admit it because of fear—fear of disrespecting God or being looked at sideways by man.

Well, babes, the Word tells us to worship God in spirit and in truth (John 4:24, KJV), and I'm here today to spill all the tea on how religion jacked me up—but more importantly, to tell you about the triumphant God who came to deliver me!

The enemy only has one agenda—to keep you from knowing who you are in Christ. He knows that once you get that revelation within, you will **stomp** him in the face and chase after all that God has for you.

Beloved, you will never know who you are—let alone *be* who you are in Christ—without a relationship with Him. This freedom journey has taught me who I am in Him, and He has revealed so much about me to me that I now have enough information to run the race He has set before me (Hebrews 12:1, NIV).

I'd like to share just a few of the names God calls me—so you'll know that He's waiting to reveal the same about you, too.

The **GREAT I AM** says, **I AM** a Kingdom Financier, Business Coach, Prophetic Intercessor, Watchman, Creative, Quartermaster, Standard Bearer, Kingdom Sniper, Deliverance Minister, Repairer of the Breach, Wailing Woman, Arsenal for His Kingdom, Master Photographer, Credit Negotiator, Weapon of Mass Destruction, Prophetic Lawyer Girl, Frontliner, and Author with the Esther and Deborah anointing.

This ain't all—but it's enough for you to see just what having a relationship with Him has revealed. Guess what? **I am still becoming!** He told me I was an author in 2019, and here I am in 2025, releasing my first book.

It is indeed my hope that my story will ignite a desire in you and compel you to go gain your own personal revelation of who you are in Christ. My prayer is that everyone who reads this book will experience just a little more *freedom* by the time you're done. I pray that you will walk away from religion into relationship—pick up your bed and not just walk, but run freely in Him, in the mighty and matchless name of Jesus!

> May you always aim to please the audience
> of One—our Father!

God just wanted to reveal Himself as *Loving Father* to me, because He said I had only been introduced to *the Judge*. It was His overwhelming love that He began to pour out on me immediately that deepened my love for Him.

I won't say I didn't have some level of relationship with Him, because I did talk to Him—but I realize now it was a one-sided relationship where I never sat still long enough to see what He had to say. I knew quite a bit about His hand but never knew His face.

I checked the weekly box of attending church and thought that was my relationship with Him. Oh, how I was missing out—but I'm so glad He loved me enough to come get me and introduce me to His freedom.

I entered Breath of Life Church on a cane, **but today**, I stand tall in His freedom—healed, whole, set free, and delivered.

Breaking the *Good Girl* Syndrome

PART 1

THE MAKING OF A GOOD GIRL

How Religion Crafted a Mask I Couldn't Breathe Through

CHAPTER 1

Fear in a Dress: My Childhood in Religion

The million-dollar question has always been, *"What in the hell is this heaviness?"* I knew it was there, but it was almost as if it were this dirty little secret buried beneath shame—something I didn't want anyone to know about. Along with the heaviness came an internal battle with torment, self-condemnation, perfectionism, guilt, overthinking, nervousness, fear, and so much more.

The silent questions were endless: *Why am I like this? Why do I feel as though something bad is going to happen to me all the time? Why do I feel these things? Why do I feel so out of place? And could somebody please tell me why I remember a bunch of church stuff but no real "park, riding my bike, being outside" moments from my childhood?*

My first encounters with spiritual sensitivity and deliverance go way back. I remembered prophetic words that were given to the adults—words some of them forgot about—but here I was, from childhood well into adulthood, remembering them all. I remember my first encounter with deliverance like it was yesterday. I was six years old.

The lady on the floor was slithering like a snake under the pew while the adults frantically gathered all the children and pushed us into the fellowship hall. I remember having a desire to see it—and as scary as I was considered to be, that didn't scare me. I was looking back like Lot's wife, trying to see what was happening. I was intrigued. It was a combination of all these things that helped me conclude that something about me was different—and I, for one, didn't like it.

From childhood to adulthood, there were never-ending curiosities that lay beneath the surface. Life was full of questions that I wanted and needed satisfying answers to. However, oftentimes I didn't even know how to verbalize what I was feeling—much less try to articulate it to someone else. So, I covered it with a smile, learned how to be a "Good Girl," and simply followed all the rules so I could make it into heaven one day. That was the end goal.

So, how did it all begin? I was raised in a single-parent household with my mother and two siblings. I believe we had a pretty normal childhood. My mother worked very hard to provide for us, and she always made sure she left us with safe people every time she went off to work. She was very cautious and strict about who and where she would leave us because our safety was always her number-one concern—and we knew without a shadow of a doubt that she loved us. That has not changed one bit about my mother!

I come from a large family. My grandparents had eleven children, and they instilled love and Christian values in all of them. Although my mom had ten siblings, she was extremely close to one of my aunts—who was thirteen years older than her.

My mom really respected her advice, leadership, and the Christian values she lived by. My mother valued the guidance, love, and protection of my aunt and the other women of faith—aka the *Women in White*—so she often gave them many permissions into the lives of her children.

My siblings and I spent a great deal of time at my aunt's house. We all lived pretty sheltered lives with lots of rules to follow and couldn't do many things that were considered "sin." We didn't go to sports events, school functions, the movies, or play cards, because according to the adults, all those things were bad and would land us in hell. At the time, this wasn't a big deal for me because I thought it was the norm—and all the children we played with had the same thing going on. It was simply the church culture.

Even with all the rules and restrictions, I was still a happy-go-lucky, chipper, giddy child who understood what love, compassion, family unity, and treating people the way you wanted to be treated looked like at a young age.

I always enjoyed going to my aunt's house because my cousins were there, and we had lots of fun playing together. I can remember playing games like "Peanut" when we rode out with my uncle and aunt as they took care of business. I just can't leave you hanging without telling you the rules of *Peanut!* Whenever we saw a Volkswagen Beetle, the first person to yell "Peanut!" got to add it to their total count. Whoever had the most by the time we made it home won the game. The prize was absolutely nothing—we just had a ball making noise and having our good ole clean fun.

The posse included my mother's three children and my aunt's three children—the six of us were very close, like peas in a pod, raised almost like siblings.

We also played many games at home together, colored often, and attended choir rehearsal, Bible study, and church regularly—*heavy* on church, with it being the most important thing to do and place to be. This was the norm for me, and because most of the youth we encountered were doing the same things, it seemed to be everybody's norm. The church culture was all I knew, and in my eyes as a young girl, there was nothing wrong with it. This was where love was instilled in me and where I received the most love. It was also where most of my friendships were formed.

The way I saw it, we all were just trying to please this man named Jesus and make it into heaven to be with Him one day—and that sounded like a plan to me!

Indoctrinated by fear, not love, we spent a lot of time in church hearing about hell. I can remember if someone said it was hot outside, my aunt would respond with, "It's seven times hotter in hell!"—not realizing that these teachings were igniting fear and anxiety inside of me. The topic of sin was an everyday discussion, and we'd better quit everything by tomorrow because Jesus was soon to come. So, I tried with all my might to be a good girl and do everything right.

So much so that one summer, while at my grandmother's house, I was outside playing when two twins came over and started picking with me. I remember thinking I should just turn the other cheek like the Bible said, so I began to walk away in hopes they'd leave me alone. I figured if I turned the other cheek and showed them love, surely they would stop, right? Well, they didn't. They threw rocks at me, hitting me in the back of the head. I didn't even try to run—I just took the suffering all the way to my grandmother's house and cried when I got inside.

There I was, ten years old, worrying about sinning and fearful of doing something that would cause me to go to hell. It was my first encounter with peers outside of my norm—people who were mean and obviously didn't mind going to hell. I thought my response to their mistreatment was the godly way to respond —as far as I was concerned, they were the abnormal ones. Although this incident saddened me, I eventually got over it and continued life with my cousins and siblings.

As I got older, I began to realize my norm truly wasn't everyone's norm. Things that I hadn't paid attention to in elementary school began to stand out in middle school. I started to notice that some of the other kids at school could do the things we were forbidden to do—like wear pants, attend school functions, and dance!

At some point, I started to be teased and picked on for following the rules required to be with this Jesus character. For the first time in my life, *the rules* stood out to me. It was almost as if I had bitten my very own fruit of good and evil.

After all, it wasn't as if they hadn't been doing these things all along—I just hadn't noticed. My observation and attentiveness to what was going on around me became heightened, and boy, did the silent questions come. Inside, I wanted to know: *Why can they wear jewelry and pants? Why don't they have the beliefs I have? Why aren't they required to do what I'm required to do?*

The first thing I noticed was that some of the girls I was beginning to come in contact with wore pants. I began to notice all the "rules" everyone else was breaking—at least in my childlike understanding.

CHAPTER 2

When Tears Were My Voice

I was labeled as weak but spiritually aware—and get this—these were *only* the observations of the outside world. I also began to observe my inside world. Even as a child, I was very observant and attentive to my surroundings.

As I got older, I began to notice everyone else's strengths and pay close attention to the things they were praised for—their voices, their musical talents, their ability to speak in front of others during special programs at church and their boldness. I often found myself in my head or my thoughts, wondering how God was going to use me.

Everyone seemed so bold and outspoken, while all I ever did was cry. Comparing myself to others started early for me. I remember asking my aunt one day how God would use me, and she told me that God was going to use my meekness and humbleness to draw people to Him. I told her that I hated my tears and wished God would take them away. I can hear her response as if it were yesterday.

She said to me, "Tippy, God bottles up your tears, so don't ask Him to stop them."

My mother wasn't the only one who looked up to my aunt. I also loved and admired her, and her words held weight with me because of the way she honored the Lord and showed love to her family. I was so content with how she said Jesus would use me, and I didn't think so badly about my tears anymore. I was really on top of the world after that conversation—it was as if a void had been filled that I didn't even know needed filling, at a time when I had no idea what the word *void* even meant.

Her answer fed and satisfied one of those childhood curiosities, and because of my deep love for Jesus and my desire to please Him, I was full of giddiness, joy, and excitement. It certainly made me feel better about myself because, up until that point, I had felt like a weak runt with nothing to offer anyone.

Things continued to get better for me, and shortly after my aunt's words of encouragement, I began to be praised for my academic abilities as well. If *"This Little Light of Mine, I'm Gonna Let It Shine"* was a person, it surely was me—and boy, was I soaking it up! I grabbed hold of that and aimed to continue making my mother proud by excelling in school. I was proud of myself, and it truly meant the world to me.

But then came family pain, guilt, and a silenced identity. Even the one thing I was good at began to be stifled because of someone else's fear—and the decisions of the *Women in White*.

In the eighth grade, I was chosen to represent Rogers-Herr Middle School in the National Spelling Bee. I was so excited and ready, but I wasn't allowed to go because of fear that something would happen to me—and all the Women in White agreed. It was their way of protecting me, so I accepted it, but I didn't realize it was a hurt I had packed deep inside.

It was at that moment that I wanted to get away from everybody. I loved and respected them all—they were powerful in the Lord—but they were also very strict and limiting. It just seemed as though fear, disguised as protection, stopped everything. We couldn't do a thing, couldn't go anywhere, and now here they were cramping my style in the very thing I excelled in.

The next year, I started high school. I remember feeling a little nervous, but thankfully, my cousin, who was a few years older—was there. At least I had someone I knew.

Unfortunately, the following year, things took a turn. I was accused of saying something about her to someone—something I honestly didn't recall saying. To "**settle it**," the matter was *taken to the Lord in prayer* and the verdict from the Lord, <u>or so they say</u>, was that I *did* say it. My cousin was withdrawn from the school and placed in a private school.

I was heartbroken because now it felt like the Lord didn't like me, and all the encouragement I'd received from my aunt about how God would use me was now shattered. There I was, fifteen years old, thinking and feeling like the bad guy with a bad heart over something I didn't even remember saying.

I became so consumed with guilt because my cousin was hurt, and for the first time in our lives, there was a separation. Can you imagine what I was feeling? All of this—and more—

took place between the ages of thirteen and fifteen. So many heart hits as a child, back-to-back, in such a short span of time.

This child who only wanted to love and please everyone, was now being ostracized. Nonetheless, I tried to continue doing what I was taught—to love and forgive. I picked up from there as best I could, but I continued to suffer massive hurt at the hands of my family.

Not much longer after this, I became my oldest sister's target of attack. She started saying things like, "You think you're better than me," and "You're Mama's favorite." In an attempt to make her feel okay—and because of guilt—I would dumb myself down. I didn't want her to feel that way about me. I actually wanted to be close to my sister. I loved her, but I settled in my heart that she didn't want anything to do with me. Pain and rejection eventually drove us apart. This was painful because all my life, I had worked so hard to treat people the way I wanted to be treated, but for some reason, I was being made the bad guy. Because I never knew how to defend myself, I kept quiet—and tears became my voice.

Tears were my way of releasing the pain, which also brought another level of pain because I was pegged as weak. I cried so much that people expected me to, and no matter how hard I tried not to, I would fail. This caused me to condemn myself even more. Negative thoughts about myself were really taking over—all while I kept a huge smile on my face. I was broken on the inside.

Time went on, and per usual, I continued to show love the best way I could—packing these hurts along the way.

Perfectionism, Performance, and A Desire to Please Everyone—Including God

I knew from a prophetic word spoken to me at the age of twelve that God wanted to use me. Those were the exact words spoken over me as I stood in a revival line, scared to death. It made me feel seen, loved, and good because it was as if God Himself was letting me know—through a stranger—that He would use me, confirming what my aunt had told me years before.

I had no idea what all of it meant, so I just began to talk to God from my heart even more. As I got older, that word came back to mind, and new questions and curiosities arose—but so did all these strange emotions and behaviors: fear, doubt, nervousness, and anxiety leading the way.

All of "the stuff"—you know, *the stuff*—the behaviors that were the result of my environment and the indoctrination of hell-teaching, I tried so desperately to hide.

The how, what, when, where, and why of God using me was frightening, even though deep down I wanted to be used. I didn't want to mess this thing up—whatever "it" was. I didn't want to get anything wrong.

The pressures of perfectionism often took me out—causing me to faint and fold. You know the type- that person who starts moving to the background, proclaiming, *"I'm a support person; just stick me in the back and I'll be fine."* The person who dumbs themselves down to make everyone else feel comfortable? Yes—that's who I eventually settled into being.

The support system. Everything to everyone else, and

nothing to myself—somehow finding a way to make that into "the purposes of God" for my life, all while feeling void and empty, knowing I was meant for greater. And I wanted *greater!*

At sixteen, my mother asked me to go with her to the hospital to do my sister's hair. My sister had just given birth to my niece and needed help. I told my mom I didn't want to go, and I got the longest "family support speech" ever!

I can remember it like it was yesterday. "Tiffany, you know how to do hair, and when we have strengths, we use them to help others."

Although I understood what my mother was saying, it wasn't my responsibility—but to please her, I did it. And if I'm honest, there was a part of me that felt good that my mother had that kind of confidence in me. I just didn't like the guilt trips.

It was always in my heart to please my mother, and if doing my sister's hair would please her, then hair it was. After all, it lined right up with who people-pleasing was calling me to be.

As time went on, I became the "fixer of everyone's problems"—and *Captain Save-a-Hoe*. This pretty much became a way of life for me. I didn't consider it a bad thing because, after all, that's what Jesus would do, right? I mean, I was capable, and helping people was one of my strengths.

Although I didn't mind helping others, guilt began to form inside of me—guilt I shouldn't have felt but didn't know how to get rid of. Here I was, doing all I could for others, so why was I feeling guilty, even while helping them?

I found myself beginning to separate from family for the first time in my life. By now, I was choosing to work long hours and multiple days to avoid being home. School, work, extracurricular activities—you name it—if it consumed my time and kept me in a happy place mentally, I was all for it.

I was really starting to view family differently. I loved them, but I knew deep down that at the first opportunity to leave, I'd be gone. Home wasn't a bad place—it just wasn't enough anymore.

There was a yearning and deep desire for more:

- A desire to laugh more
- A desire to be around lighthearted people
- A desire to experience and be exposed to more
- A desire not to feel the fear, guilt, or anxiety that seemed to consume me

One advantage of my cousin being pulled out of school was that it gave me the chance to meet new friends. I began to blossom in a different way. I met my best friend during this time—she was unchurched and very freeing—and that, in turn, brought out the carefree part of me that had been buried deep inside.

I wanted more of that. I didn't want to feel whatever this heaviness was anymore.

It was almost time to graduate high school, and I was on cloud nine. By then, I had met so many new friends, accomplished so many academic achievements, the Women in White were passing away, and my mother's strictness was fading.

We weren't made to go to church anymore. The church we attended closed after the pastor passed, and I was so happy to be out of church. I loved Jesus—but I didn't love *church* anymore. I was just so tired of hearing about sin. I kept thinking, *There has to be more to this than the same old tired message of sin!*

I kept saying to myself, *The Bible says to preach the Gospel, and the Gospel is the Good News of Jesus Christ—not sin!*

My motto became: *Leave people alone. People know when they're messing up—they don't need anyone reminding them about their sin!*

It was so nerve-wracking to me. But I was older now, and it was time for me to find Jesus for myself. I was all for it because I was finally free—from the rules, from control, from anyone telling me what to do or how to live my life.

Then came the big day. On June 6, 1989, I graduated with honors from Durham High School, home of the mighty Bulldogs—ending the '80s in style at the tender age of seventeen!

I was ready to explore all the things this little sheltered girl thought she had missed out on—but deep down, there was still the matter of Jesus. I loved Him, I wanted Him, but it all still felt too heavy, too hard, and too suffocating.

CHAPTER 3

Raised by Rules, Not Relationship

Legalism, False Reverence and Transactional Theology

Everything led back to God in a *religious* way—so much so that I felt guilty for wanting or desiring to do more, have more, and become more. I mean, even the mention of exercising gained negative feedback because exercise was fine, but I was told I needed to "get my spirit man right." *Sheesh!*

So many rules to follow. So many do's and don'ts. And although the *Women in White* had faded, and I was no longer being made to go to church, there was still this never-ending, echoing voice on the inside telling me all the things I was doing wrong—and all the things I wasn't and never would be.

So, I made it a point to just continue being the overachieving good girl so no one would have anything bad to say about Tiffany.

- *If I do this, then I'll get that.*
- *If I act this way, everyone will love me.*
- *If I stay quiet and out of the way, no one will bother me.*
- *If I follow this rule, then God won't punish me.*
- *If I obey Him, then He'll give me something good.*
- *If they do this, then I must do that.*
- *Can I have this if I give you that?*
- *Will you do this for me if I do that for you?*

One transaction after another—showing up in every relationship.

It became such a part of me that I didn't even know how to allow anyone to do anything for me without feeling obligated to do something in return. And when those opportunities did occur, I was overly thankful and appreciative, as if I didn't deserve it.

If I continued to turn the other cheek and say yes to everyone—doing exactly what they wanted—then surely God would be pleased. If I sacrificed my well-being for the well-being of others, then surely I would make it into Heaven and God would love me.

Before I knew it, a long trail of **transactional living** had been birthed—with family, friends, and even God—and I was well on my way to living a life of lies, where every *no* I wanted to say became a *yes*.

There was an internal battle raging within me. I was fighting to remain that giddy, outgoing, carefree person—but there was another person screaming to take over: the person religion had taught me to be. *She wore the mask just to survive.*

The very opposite of what I desired was happening to me, and the most I could do was keep a smile on my face—then cry secretly when no one was watching. I became angry with everyone, angry with myself, and low-key angry with God.

This was all the more reason to bail out.

I was torn between wanting to have fun and wanting to go to Heaven. So, for a while, I chose to have fun—leaving the church behind to be free from it all.

For me, it had to be one or the other because there was just too much guilt, too much shame, and too much feeling like a hypocrite to keep attending church every Sunday while I wanted to just have fun in what the saints called *sin*.

Chile, don't even fix your brain to think this was easy—because it wasn't. It came with massive guilt, shame, and a constant fear of dying before I could make it back.

Religion Taught Me How to be Broke, Invisible, and Afraid

Ages seventeen to twenty-two were pivotal years in my life. These years covered my senior year in high school through my first year of motherhood. By the time I graduated, I didn't want any more schooling—which was shocking to everyone.

Say what? Tiffany's not going to college? **NOPE!**

I was just trying to be free from what everyone else wanted me to do, and at the time, it felt like the perfect plan—until the summer ended and all my friends went off to start the next chapters of their lives. Meanwhile, I—**Miss Top Ten** in her class—didn't have a plan in sight.

Some went into the military while others went off to college, near and far. So here I was, bored, with nothing to do but work. "Train up a child in the way they should go" Proverbs 22:6, (KJV), didn't seem to make it past the church doors, so planning any future outside of what I had seen within my own environment was never part of the plan—or maybe it was, and I just kept dumbing myself down to be liked and make everyone else comfortable with me.

However, the following year, out of pure boredom, I decided to attend school and work part-time. Although my body was no longer in the church building, my mind was still enslaved to the bondage of religion and everything it had taught me.

We were taught not to store treasures up here on earth but to lay them up in heaven Matthew 6:19–20, (KJV). We were told that you couldn't serve both God and mammon Matthew 6:24, (KJV), and somehow, **struggle + broke = super anointed**—as if being poor was proof you were truly making a sacrifice unto Jesus.

This chick still wanted more—but was too afraid to do something different, because I didn't want to hear that I "thought I was better."

All I knew, in this silent mind of mine, was that I desired more money—not for selfish gain, but to be a blessing to the church.

Because honestly, I was tired of trying to figure out why all these grown folks only had a few dollars to put in the collection plate!

I mean, there was always an announcement that "we need more money to meet our goal," yet the same people shouting, *"You can't serve God and mammon!"* never had any real money to give—then turned around and begged for more money *at every service.*

When the plate came around the second time, all the loose change came out!

If "make it make sense" was a person, back then—it would've been me. But y'all know children didn't have a say in those days, so I kept quiet and continued to pretend I was okay—all while the circling thought, *"There has to be more to Jesus than this,"* stayed at the forefront of my mind.

Wearing a mask became survival...

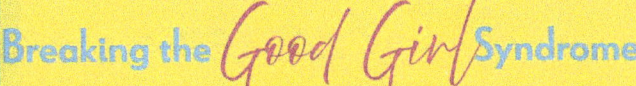

Breaking the *Good Girl* Syndrome

PART 2

THE COLLAPSE OF CONTROL

What Happens When You Realize Religion Isn't Healing You

CHAPTER 4

The High Cost of Trying to Be Good

I never knew that being good could cost me so much. Everything I shared in the last few chapters was real—but I didn't understand how much it had cost me until I reached a breaking point.

I spent the majority of my early years trying to embody the image of the perfect daughter, the perfect niece, and the perfect church girl. And still, I found myself wounded by the very people I loved most—misunderstood, accused, and labeled in ways that didn't reflect my heart.

The cost of being good wasn't just exhaustion—it was identity loss, emotional suppression, and betrayal by the ones I never thought would harm me.

Not to mention the pain associated with *turning the other cheek*. I never stood up for myself because I believed that standing up for myself meant I was being mean to someone—and that God would "get me" for it. So, I learned how to take the blame.

I learned how to come into agreement with lies just to keep the peace.

I learned how not to value myself and to put everyone else first.

I learned to suppress and accept all the negative things spoken about me.

I learned that I didn't matter.

And worst of all, I learned to believe the lies—of the enemy, of others, and of myself.

Family Betrayal and Accusations

I was accused of things I never remembered saying. I was forced to carry guilt for pain I didn't cause. When conflict arose in my family—especially among those I loved dearly—it was easier for them to label me than to understand me.

There was one moment in particular when I was just a teenager, and my cousin was withdrawn from school based on a claim that I had said something about her. I had no recollection of the incident, and instead of having a conversation, the matter was "taken to the Lord in prayer."

The result? I was found guilty—by prayer, not truth.

That experience shattered me. I wasn't just hurt—I was spiritually condemned.

I had been the good girl—the one who followed the rules, never rebelled, always aimed to please—and yet, in one sweeping moment, that entire image collapsed under the weight of someone else's assumption and spiritual authority.

It broke my heart and shook the foundation of my faith. I questioned my worth, my integrity, and even my ability to hear from God.

Dumbing Down for Approval

The betrayal didn't stop there. My sister—older and troubled in her own right—began projecting her pain onto me. She would accuse me of being our mother's favorite and constantly make snide remarks that made me feel like my accomplishments were weapons against her rather than signs of growth.

In an attempt to keep the peace, I dimmed my light. I dumbed myself down. I stopped celebrating my wins and buried my voice so she wouldn't feel threatened by me.

I learned early on how to shrink to survive.

The irony? I wasn't trying to be better than anyone. I was just trying to be good. I was trying to be helpful, kind, honest. But when you're surrounded by people who are hurting, even your goodness can be interpreted as an offense.

The weight of constantly managing other people's feelings—while suffocating your own—turned me into a silent sufferer. I gave until I was empty and apologized for existing in rooms I was called to fill.

Performance-Driven Guilt and Shame

Over time, I became the one everyone called on to fix things, to pray, to serve, to give, to show up. And I did—every single time. But somewhere along the line, my giving stopped being pure. I wasn't giving because I wanted to; I was giving because I didn't know how to say no. I feared that setting a boundary would make me selfish.

I feared that if I didn't help, I would be abandoned or seen as less spiritual. My service was no longer worship—it was performance. And that performance cost me my peace, my confidence, and my emotional well-being.

I cried more than I spoke. I was pegged as "too sensitive," "too emotional," or just flat-out weak. But what they didn't understand was that my tears were the language of my survival.

They were the only way I could release what I had no permission to express.

For years, I smiled while dying inside. I served while suffocating. I complied while quietly questioning everything. The cost of being good wasn't holiness—it was heartbreak.

But what I didn't know then is that God wasn't looking for a perfect little girl in a white dress. He was waiting for the broken woman in the corner to call out His name. He wasn't after my performance—He wanted my permission to come into the mess and rescue me from the pressure I was never designed to carry.

This chapter marks the turning point. The undoing. The moment I began to realize that goodness without freedom isn't righteousness—it's bondage dressed up in church clothes.

CHAPTER 5

Deliverance or Disguise?

Toxic relationships and spiritual control

Eventually, thoughts of church—and all things church—faded away. By this point, I hadn't been a member of anyone's church since the age of sixteen, and here I was at nineteen, continuously ramping up "my fun life" by way of the club, which is where I met my daughter's father. We hit it off on day one, and he became my boyfriend. We both loved to dance, we both loved reggae, and we both loved the club—the perfect match, right?

Later, I was hired by a photographer who worked several clubs located in Durham and Raleigh. I was in my element with the camera—scoring free entry into the clubs, snapping as many personal polaroids for myself as I did for customers—with my childhood best friend, Tabitha, and my boyfriend right there by my side. I was having the time of my life—but then it happened.

A year later, I got pregnant and gave birth to my daughter, Jamesha, in 1992 at the age of twenty-one. Sometime between finding out I was pregnant and her birth, church began circling my mind. I knew I wanted to raise my daughter in church because I needed and wanted her to know God, so I decided to start my journey of looking for the "right" church suitable for me.

I started attending Greenway Baptist Church[2] with my daughter's godmother. It was a little more freeing than what I was used to. People wore pants, makeup, and jewelry to church—which was a NO-NO in the Holiness church. There wasn't much shouting like I was used to, but the people seemed lighthearted in comparison to what I knew, and that's what I needed—something light. I had a few friends there and liked the church overall, so I became a regular attendee. My daughter was dedicated back to God while I attended; however, I never joined and eventually left.

Not too much longer after that, her father and I broke up, and I found myself heartbroken with a new baby. He wasn't the first to cause me heartbreak, but something about that breakup affected me in a way my previous relationships had not. I found myself getting into one relationship right after another, entangling myself in a web of men—looking for love in all the wrong places.

Now before you get any bright ideas—I wasn't a promiscuous woman. I was loyal in my relationships and dedicated to who I was with. But when the relationship was over, I never looked back. The problem was, I never gave myself time to heal. I simply moved on to the next qualified recipient to receive this "fixer" love. The love and compassion I had for those I loved was something I didn't fully understand. I just knew it ran deep—and because of it, I suffered many deep hurts.

---

[2] The Church Name has been changed to protect the integrity of the work of the Lord that is being completed through the vessels that serve as the Founders of this Faith-based Institution.

During this era, the "fixer" inside of me grew, and it seemed like every man I encountered was a project of potential that I became a ride-or-die chick for. I was proud to be needed, depended on, used, and abused—all in the name of love. And let's not get it twisted—it was indeed love, a perverted love that needed cleansing.

Eventually, the Lord began to draw me to Him, and I could no longer live without Him in my life, so I set out again to find a church suitable for me. I knew I still wanted something different than what I was raised in, but I didn't know what that looked like because all I had ever been part of was deliverance ministries. I started attending a church in Durham, NC, with an associate. The people were great, the services were exciting, but—get this—it also reminded me a little of my upbringing, just not to the tenth power.

I eventually joined and found myself satisfied and settled. I had finally found a church that didn't make me feel bound by—and to—hell. The unadulterated Word was still being preached, but there wasn't a focus on hell.

One particular Sunday, nearing the end of service, my pastor went into his office and came back out with a trash can—and I immediately was like, "Awww h*** naw," lol. Y'all, please tell me why I joined a deliverance ministry and didn't even know it! I should've figured out right then that Deliverance Ministries and I apparently had a thing going on—yet, no one sent me the memo. I was too done, BUT I loved the church, so, I stayed a bit.

Eventually, I left because of the messiness I'd never seen in church. Sure, they had been strict in my upbringing, but at least they didn't play with division, gossip, slander, or foolishness. Seeing all that for the first time in church?

Yeah, I was immediately turned off. There I was—out of church again, and "out of the protection of God," as we'd been taught—but this time, I wasn't as worried. I knew I'd eventually find another one. I just didn't want to be there anymore.

Life began to life, and before I knew it, I drifted away from my desire to attend church. I became engulfed in work, just trying to make a living for me and my baby. For a while it was just she and I, without a boyfriend in sight. I was getting older and desired someone who was on the same page—someone who, even if they weren't where they wanted to be yet, was at least striving to get there, not men who watched me work, pay all the bills, and chill without a goal or plan.

Three years passed, and the next serious relationship I found myself in was with my son's father. I met him in August of 1998, introduced by his cousin—straight out of prison on parole. Lawd, girl! She said her cousin was cool and relocating to NC for a fresh start, and she wanted him to meet one of her friends so they could hang out during a family movie night. She thought my personality would be better for the job. I agreed—after all, the plan was for all of us to hang out at the movies, right? WRONG! The entire family canceled, and the two of us ended up hanging out together—and the rest was history.

Things started out really well, and we became a couple. Jamesha absolutely loved him, and I loved how he treated her. I loved how he gave me insight on things based on their conversations. He was very good with girls, having helped raise his nieces. He was protective over her, and I appreciated that finally one of these men showed interest in my daughter's well-being.

As time went on, he reconnected with people he once knew from a previous time in NC and, unfortunately, violated his parole. He was shipped back to Philadelphia, PA, to finish out his bid, and I vowed to wait for him and support him in any way I could. He only had a year left, which wasn't long, but the day he left I was so sad—yet determined to show him a love he had never seen.

I wrote him every single day, kept money on his books, sent pictures, and spoke life to him. I treated him with kindness and respect regardless of his situation, and I know that's what truly won his heart. His treatment was so good the other men were jealous. He told me they hated when the mail came because his name was called every day. I loved that for him—and I loved how it made him feel.

For me, it was always about making people feel good about themselves, and I thrived in that because—guess what—it also stroked the ego of the people pleaser, the one who needed the approval of man, the fixer, and the good girl.

Six months into his bid—here comes Jesus drawing me. If I'm honest, I wasn't as eager to go this time. I was enjoying myself, and I wasn't ready to put the dresses back on, take the earrings off, or settle back into that dull, rigid person that came with trying to follow all those rules. Not to mention, doing so was about to cramp my style with this man.

Although the last two churches I attended didn't push the rules as hard, "the rules" were so deeply embedded in me that I chose to follow them to reverence and honor the Lord every time I stepped into anyone's church. As I set out to find a church, I shared with Luffy[3] that God was drawing me and explained

---

[3] Name has been changed to protect the privacy of the individual involved.

what that meant. He was glad, because he felt it would be good for him to start attending church as well when he returned.

Tithing was something I did faithfully, whether I belonged to a church or not. I had $200 I wanted to tithe somewhere and asked God to give me a sign of where to give. Later that evening, driving down Roxboro Rd. in Durham, I saw my aunt with my uncle and two cousins in their van. I started waving and blowing the horn from afar. The closer I got, it looked like a slow-motion movie scene. I was blowing and waving to get their attention, and they all looked straight ahead and never saw me. We were on opposite sides of the road in the lanes closest to one another, so they should've seen me. I took that as a sign to take the money to my aunt, so I called, and made arrangements.

The False Start of Rededication and Return to Religion

When I got there, what was supposed to be me just dropping off some money turned into an extensive conversation—and an agreement to start attending their home church. INSERTS SCREAM !!!

This was the first time I'd been around them like this since my cousin was removed from the high school we attended together and sent to private school. I loved my aunt and my family, but I did not want to return to the "hell teaching" on the level I knew I was about to endure. The good girl in me didn't know how to say that—or to tell her I'd changed my mind.

There was also a part of me that felt like this must be God's will, so I rededicated my life to Christ and started the very next Sunday. I immediately fell right back under the rules, and slowly but surely, the life was zapped out of me. I found myself trying to be two people: the carefree individual I had been up to this point and the individual who wore the mask to survive—misery at its best.

I shared everything with Luffy and quickly found out he wasn't going for it. He was cool when I told him I was changing the way I dressed and even cool about me not wearing jewelry—but he drew the line at **we** would not be able to listen to secular music. He was musically talented and didn't believe it was a sin to listen to secular music—particularly R&B, which he loved. He wasn't rude and didn't try to turn me away from God, but he did tell me it sounded like I was in a cult—and boy, did I get fish-grease hot and mad.

Nobody could talk about my aunt or anything concerning her to me, because I knew she loved the Lord and genuinely loved people. Although conflict arose between us, the relationship continued because he wasn't going anywhere—he just wasn't agreeing that he couldn't listen to Earth, Wind & Fire, Larry Graham, and he definitely wasn't giving up George Clinton.

At that moment, the little freedom I did have in sharing my journey with him left the building, and I began to slip back into masking, pretending, and people-pleasing. Just when I thought it couldn't get worse, my cousins began to tell me I had to put my roommate out because she listened to secular music in my house—and if I continued to allow her to stay, I was in disobedience to God.

In an effort to keep the peace, I asked her not to play secular music anymore because of my beliefs, and she agreed; however, my family would not let up. I was caught between a rock and a hard place. I didn't want to put her out, but I didn't want to be in disobedience either.

I stalled as long as I could—until one day I came home and heard the music playing as I pulled into the yard. I used the frustration and anger from the pressure I felt "to do right by God" to tell her she had to leave. She was devastated, and I felt so guilty for doing that to my friend. She left within the week and never spoke to me again.

When I shared it with Luffy, he didn't understand or agree, which heightened the guilt I was already feeling. If I'm honest, I didn't understand myself—especially why I couldn't at least give her time. It felt cruel, but I didn't know how to say no or voice disagreement. Because of the respect and honor I had for my aunt and cousins, I didn't believe they would lead me wrong. In my eyes, they were still the ones who could hear the Lord better than I could and would never intentionally hurt anyone.

Here I was again—allowing my life to be controlled by someone else, but now in my adult life. Not only that—the heaviness came back, and I began to feel the same bondage I had worked so hard to escape in my youth.

As far as I was concerned, I was the bad guy and couldn't face my friend or her family. So, I did what I knew how to do: I packed the guilt and the hurt of hurting someone else.

Of course, I moved forward—but soon after, I was hit with another bomb of bondage. It was nearing time for Luffy to get out of prison. With only two months left to complete his time and be free from parole, his name came up in a conversation with my cousins. They told me I couldn't be with him and that "the Lord said" he would never amount to anything.

My heart sank. I was perplexed—full of fear, doubt, anger, and frustration. You see, my aunt and cousins, who never left home, had dedicated their entire lives to serving Jesus, so when they said something about "living right" and being obedient, it carried weight with me. I was too afraid to offend them—I equated them with being God's representatives, and they were never wrong.

I was heartbroken because Luffy had already acknowledged he wanted to start going to church, and I was eager for him to meet my family when he returned. I couldn't bring myself to tell him what "the Lord" had said about him. I hoped that when he got out and started attending church with me, they would see he was a cool dude.

The time came. He was released, and we both attended an evening program at church together on Easter Sunday. I remember it like yesterday—we arrived, and I introduced him to my family. They greeted him and showed love.

The program started, and everything was fine at first—just your typical service. Then, out of nowhere, one of my cousins started praising God. Next thing I know, right in the middle of her praise, she breaks out with this prophetic word of rebuke, yelling, "You can't hide!" It was loud, sharp, and aimed straight at me—one of the harshest words I'd ever heard, all about me being with Luffy and planning to move out of Durham. At first, I felt guilty; then I felt angry—because *what do you mean I can't hide,* as if I was running from them? Excuse me, but God already knows where I'm going. The anger was followed by sadness.

I felt bad for Luffy because there was nothing slow about him—he knew he'd been discussed prior to coming home.

I was embarrassed and over it. What really took the cake was when I was informed I would have to give back all the certificates I'd received from their ministry if I remained "in disobedience" with Luffy. I had no intention of leaving the church, but I was

too done—not "done, I'm leaving," but done as in another hurt I had to pack because I was being excommunicated. They showed me Scripture to support what they were doing, and because I refused to continue being controlled, I accepted my "punishment," returned the certificates, and left—but not before they told me I would suffer for my disobedience, laying another layer of guilt and shame on me as I exited.

An Abusive Marriage, Substance Use, and the Cry for Freedom

Luffy and I continued in our relationship, which started off really well—until we secured our first apartment together. He reconnected with old friends, lost his job, and relapsed. My life quickly took a drastic turn from what I was used to in relationships—but never fear, Captain Save-a-Hoe was here.

I had no idea what I was doing, but I knew I loved him enough to stick by his side. He was more than drugs to me. I had seen his heart, his potential, his kindness, and his faithfulness, and I believed it was my job to help him get back on his feet as his ride-or-die chick.

The relationship became an abusive one—and I even made excuses for that. *It's the drugs,* I told myself—because before the drugs, he was so sweet. *If he could just stop, everything would be okay*.

The next few years were a rollercoaster—sober one minute, not the next—with jail time entering the picture. Every release came with a promise to do better, and he did, for a while—until the cycle returned.

Long story short, in April of 2002, I ended up marrying a man who was abusive and addicted to drugs—because I loved him, didn't see myself going anywhere, and believed it was "better to marry than to burn" (I Corinthians 7:9, KJV). I also thought I could love the drugs out of him. I didn't see myself as an abused woman because I fought back and there were never any scars.

I was his ride-or-die—until I got tired. I began making demands, letting him know I was done with the lifestyle of abuse, drugs, and jail. I told him if he went back to jail one more time, I was leaving. He got locked up again—and I kept my promise, but not before one last fight that caused me to walk away for good.

That fight got totally out of hand, and for the first time, I knew I was a battered woman. The "scar" I never saw turned out to be a torn muscle in my right eyelid. During the fight, he pushed me—I lost my balance, fell, and hit my eye on the corner of a wooden nightstand. We both were devastated. He was apologetic, trying to help me up off the floor as I swung at him. I made him leave, and he did—because he knew he'd messed up. I knew I was done; I couldn't even open my right eye.

Later that night, in the wee hours, I got up to use the bathroom, and something nudged me to look out my front door window. I turned on the porch light, and there he was—on the porch, looking crazy. For the first time, I was truly afraid of him. The police came, and I ended up in a battered women's shelter. After this incident, my husband and I separated.

I became friends with a woman named Roxi, who I met at the shelter, and started dating someone new. Later, I let her and my new boo stay with me because they both had their own personal issues. It was supposed to be temporary until they got on their feet.

"Tip the Savior" came up with a plan: buy some weed, sell it, get my investment back, and give them the rest. Guess what—that didn't work because we all smoked weed. Then the new boo suggested we "try crack ," and I agreed—with one condition: I wouldn't have anything to do with it, because I had suffered enough trying to save my soon-to-be ex-husband. He agreed. I gave him the money to purchase a package; he did—but it took him forever to get rid of it. I didn't know much, but based on my ex-husband's actions, it didn't take that long to get rid of no crack. Long story short—the two of them were smoking it and stealing from me.

By now, I had suffered enough with this drug—especially for someone who didn't use it. I was so mad. I had no idea he smoked. This is when I learned the difference between a functional and a non-functional addict. I said out of my mouth, "I don't even understand why people act that way over crack, because I've tried it before in a blunt and all it did was make me horny."

Roxi replied, "That's because it affects you differently on the stem than in a blunt," and asked if I wanted to try it. In an effort to prove it was "mind over matter," I agreed to try it on the stem—and off to the races I went, at thirty-four years old, battling a crack cocaine addiction.

I eventually put her and him out of my life, but struggled with the addiction for a while. Eight months in, I decided to move back to Durham, thinking if I got around my mother I would stop—but that didn't happen.

I tried rehab twice but couldn't receive what I needed, because they said things I didn't agree with—like "once an addict, always an addict," or that I'd have to fight it the rest of my life because part of the brain would always desire it. And I certainly wasn't saying, "Hi, my name is Tiffany, and I'm a recovering addict." Something inside me would not allow that confession. Not so! My mom would always tell me, "Tiffany, your deliverance is in God."

Three and a half years into addiction, after being really tired of the cycle—guess who came for me again? Yep, you got it—Jesus began to draw me, and boy, did I want Him. Between the abuse, life beating me down, and my run with addiction, it had been almost nine years since I'd been in a church for anything other than a funeral. The conviction grew stronger and stronger, but so did the hesitation—the fear of being judged and the fear of all things church.

Nonetheless, one Sunday I finally attended my cousin's church, and as she was speaking, she said, "No matter what you are going through, the Word says we are to call those things that are not as though they be" (Romans 4:17, KJV).

That word penetrated my heart. I left church, and for the next three weeks, as I went to purchase crack, I proclaimed , "I AM DELIVERED."

Then it happened—completely out of nowhere. One night, I bought some with the plan to go home and just chill by myself. I didn't invite anyone over because I wanted to enjoy it without anyone trying to ruin my high just to get me to buy more. I took a hit and fell to my knees with an expectation like none I had ever felt before, and I began to cry out to God:

"Lord, I know who You are, and Your Word says that faith without works is dead (James 2:17, KJV). Your Word also says we are to call those things that are not as though they be (Romans 4:17, KJV). So, to show You I'm serious, here's the work I'm going to put with my faith: when I get up, I am taking all this paraphernalia outside and throwing it in the big dumpster—because I know if I put it in the kitchen trash can, I'll just go back for it. And I call my deliverance from crack cocaine now, in Jesus' name."

I got up, took all that stuff outside, threw it in the dumpster, came back in the house, and got in bed. When I share this testimony, I always say: I don't know if He did it while I was on my knees, walking to the dumpster, or through the night as I slept—but when I woke up the next day, all urges were gone, and I have never struggled with—or desired—crack since. BUT GOD, y'all—did you hear what I said?

The next morning, my routine shifted and changed forever. At 10 a.m.—my usual time to get my first hit—there wasn't a single urge in sight. I was delivered instantly by God, never to be entangled again with that yoke of bondage (Galatians 5:1, KJV).

I called my deliverance using Romans 4:17—*we are to call those things that are not as though they are* (KJV)—and I will never forget it.

A brand-new day. A rescue from my Father. An answered prayer. A drug-free Tiffany. And now, it was time to get my life back on track.

CHAPTER 6

Leaving Church, Not Christ

Ten Years of "Absence" and the Torment of Guilt

But wait—it had been ten years since I'd attended church regularly. And although I wanted Jesus, I didn't want the heaviness associated with church. By this point, I had figured out that whatever that heaviness was, it was tied to all the things I'd learned in church about "trying to live right." I just didn't want to be a part of that anymore.

How do you tell yourself—or anyone for that matter—that you don't want to go to church without indirectly saying you don't want God? This was indeed my thought process because, to not be a member of a church was equivalent to not being saved or "in Christ."

However, God had just done a miraculous, spontaneous thing by delivering me from crack cocaine, and I owed Him my life—mind, body, soul, and spirit.

Two months later, I rededicated my life back to Christ and started attending church on a regular basis again. Once again, I was back to religion and all the heaviness that it brought. But the difference this time was, no matter what, I was determined to stay. Even with all the warped perceptions of Him, I wasn't going anywhere, because He had saved and rescued me in a way I had never experienced—and I knew it was nobody BUT GOD!

Here I was, starting over again, but there was one loose end that needed to be tied up. So, one day I asked God, *What do I do with this man I had no business marrying?*

Luffy had resurfaced and claimed he wanted to work things out. I didn't see myself with him, but we had a son together, and I thought maybe we could at least learn how to do healthy co-parenting. He began to come around more consistently and even attend church with me here and there. He wanted a relationship, but I was torn. Could this be him changing for the better? Was there hope years later for us?

I had seen the good, the bad, and the ugly, but I believed that God could change anyone who desired to be changed. I didn't usually go backward in relationships, but I was willing to save my marriage if I could. I didn't marry to divorce, and according to Matthew 19:9 (KJV), it was forbidden by God. So, I allowed him to be around us—but I asked the Lord to show me a sign.

The very next day, I went to meet him at the barbershop. We started arguing, and before I knew it, he shoved his arm in the window, trying to hit me with an umbrella. I took off, his arm still caught in the window, but he yanked it out just before he became roadkill. Then he chased after the car, slamming the umbrella against my back passenger-side window—shattering the glass right beside his son! OH NAW—thank You, Lord! I'm done. I'm filing for divorce.

Or so I thought.

I began to wrestle with the idea of divorce because Luffy had been faithful, and according to the Word, abuse wasn't grounds for divorce. Then I wrestled with the thought of becoming an adulterer—because adulterers would not enter the Kingdom of Heaven (I Corinthians 6:9–10, KJV). Then I wondered if I could ever remarry—or would I have to wait for him to die, as if I was sure he'd go first. There was some serious torment going on regarding this marriage and divorce. I literally picked up several divorce packets, starting the process of filling them out, but guilt would not let me finish. **BUT GOD**!

New to rededication, I needed a Bible. So, I went to the thrift store to search their book bin for one. I stuck my hand in the bin four times, and right before I reached down the fifth time, I said to myself, *If I don't grab a Bible this time, I'm just going to leave*.

I stuck my arm down as far as it would go, and the book I pulled out was titled *May I Remarry*. OMGGG—I ran to the register so fast to purchase that book so I could get my answer!

I had seen remarriage quite a few times among the adults I grew up around, but there was a guilt inside me that wouldn't even let me be great. I got home and immediately opened the book. The author talked about the very scripture I had been wrestling with, wondering whether I was supposed to stay in the marriage.

He said many women stayed in abusive relationships because they were trying to honor that scripture—but God would never want you to stay with someone who mistreats you.

He talked about the Ten Commandments—particularly, "Thou shalt not kill" (Exodus 20:13, KJV)—explaining that this didn't apply only to physical death, but also that physical abuse kills you spiritually and mentally. He then referenced the two commandments Jesus added—especially, "Love thy neighbor as thyself" (Matthew 22:39, KJV)—which indicates we are to love ourselves first. If you're allowing someone to mistreat you through physical abuse, you're not loving yourself.

I thanked God, closed the book, and went to pick up another divorce packet—which I was finally able to complete. My divorce was finalized on December 4, 2009—one of the most emotional days of my life.

It felt like failure, but God had to permit it to happen this way to set me free. That was the very first inkling I ever had that maybe—just maybe—some scriptures are interpreted incorrectly in other ways too. I was deeply saddened because my marriage was over, but I felt at peace moving forward with the divorce.

Still Believing—but Suffocating Under Spiritual Obligation

I started attending my cousin's church but wasn't as eager to join as I had been in the past. My cousin was raised by the same people I was, so I knew that although she wasn't as rigid as her sisters and mother, she still looked like—and reminded me of—all my childhood experiences with church and "the rules."

And for that reason, I knew the heaviness was somewhere around the corner waiting to get me.

I wrestled with zeal, obligation, guilt, overthinking, anxiety, self-condemnation, torment, and fear—all with a smile on my face. I even began serving as an usher before I officially joined.

I felt spiritually obligated to *do something* for the Lord because He had done something for me.

Don't get me wrong—it wasn't a daunting task. I loved serving as unto the Lord, and I loved pleasing Him. But I couldn't seem to separate the love I had for Him from this weight of heaviness that would always resurface at some point during my walk.

No one ever talked about these things, so I thought it was just me—which made me feel even worse. I eventually joined my cousin's church and dove headfirst into doing all I could to help the ministry. Then it happened—someone finally spoke on *the heaviness*—and I cried because I knew at that point I wasn't crazy.

We had an evening service, and I remember it like it was yesterday. Pastor Robert L. Mason from Greater Love Worship Center was preaching, and there I was, sitting on the front row—partially present. My body was in the seat, and I could hear every word, but my mind? It was all over the place. I had been delivered, yes, but now I was faced with cleanup. As Pastor Mason preached, I kept noticing him looking at me. My mind was already racing a mile a minute, and his staring sped it up, adding a whole new set of thoughts. I pulled myself together and refocused, tuning back into the message, distraction-free.

As Pastor Mason began to close out his sermon, he said, *"Young lady, the Lord has been speaking to me about you all night."* Whew—that explained why he kept looking at me!

He continued, saying he heard the Lord say there was a heaviness on me—and that the weight of it was equivalent to a house sitting on my shoulders. Out came the waterfall from my eyes, because someone had finally acknowledged this thing I had been wrestling with all my life—yet there was still no name for it.

Pastor Mason prophesied that within seven days, the weight would be lifted, and he prayed for me. I left church that night knowing *the Lord sees me*, and that alone gave me the strength to carry on.

Still, the question remained: *What is this heaviness?*

It was the thing that would cause me to moonwalk right out of the church when my sin got too heavy. It was the thing that caused me to battle within. It was the thing that seemed to keep me from getting to Jesus the way the depth of my soul desired to—but it still had no other name than *heavy*.

Per usual, for the next three years as a member of my cousin's church, I continued to serve the Lord with all my heart, treat others the way I wanted to be treated, and aim to please the audience of One.

My time there came to an end in 2012 due to irreconcilable family issues, so I left to join my mother's church—because remember, **I wasn't leaving God this time**. I was welcomed by everyone and made to feel at home, so the transition was easy despite the biggest family hurt and pain I had just endured.

I hadn't been there a solid two weeks when one afternoon, at the end of service, the Pastor walked up to me and said, *"Stop taking the blame for everything,"* and kept it moving—no explanation, no conversation!

I lightly chuckled, because that's all I had ever done—take the blame for every single thing that went wrong concerning me.

I knew that was God yet again showing me He sees me. In my eyes, I was simply turning the other cheek and treating people the way I wanted to be treated—despite how they treated me—not knowing God never intended for me to be a doormat.

Nonetheless, I was still rocking with Jesus—from one building to the next.

I was already familiar with the members of my mother's church because we had attended some of the same revivals and convocations during my childhood and early adult life. My mother had eventually joined this church and had been there for years. It was just another family church—which was cool.

But then came the temptation and the test—a boyfriend!

I had intentionally decided not to see anyone after I divorced Luffy because my divorce broke my heart, and I was tired of the cycle—rolling from one relationship to another. I was tired of fornication and tired of doing things my own way, continually causing my own pain. My love for Jesus was so strong, and I talked to Him often about me—and I made that known to the new boyfriend.

I told him upfront there would be no sex. I was not fornicating. No, I just wasn't!

Well, I did—and the self-condemnation and judgment began. Then came the fear of thinking something bad was going to happen.

For the first time, I stayed within the church walls because, again, I wasn't leaving Jesus. I was determined to make it through the torment, fright, and fear of what would happen if I stayed in this sin.

The good thing about the new boo was he wanted marriage, he wanted family, and he wanted to serve God—but he had a serious lust and faithfulness problem. Cheating was a dealbreaker for me on any level, but I got swindled into looking right past it as he confessed it was his weakness and repented for the lustful spirits in him.

Guess who showed up? *Ride-or-die, Captain Sav-a-hoe,* with a loud, "*Awwww, I got you in prayer, baby!*" LOL!

I didn't backslide, but I couldn't enjoy that relationship either—not at first. It became difficult to take communion because I never felt worthy of it.

I began to shrink back into this ball of nerves, wondering what Jesus was going to do. I continued in the relationship until one day I threatened to leave him—and saw a side of him I had never seen before.

He held me hostage in my own house and threatened to kill me. He even came at me with a butcher knife, knocking me out of my office chair onto the floor, then getting on top of me and stabbing the floor beside my head with the knife.

He thought what he thought—but found out quickly that ya girl wasn't doing *another* domestic violence relationship.

He was very sorrowful, and I was very shocked. My Pastor was disappointed in what had taken place because he really loved having him as a member. But now, there was friction. The boo eventually left the church, but not too long after that, I was right back with him. Although the violence never happened again, the next few years with him were filled with turmoil, drama, lies, and sin. Blue and I eventually broke up.

I was broken yet again—picking up the pieces to move forward while my life seemed to take a hit one thing at a time. And while I blamed myself, self-condemnation multiplied to the point that I stopped taking communion, even after I had repented and ended the relationship.

One Sunday, as my Pastor preached his sermon, he made several points using biblical examples of people who had gone through what he saw each of his members experiencing. He went around the room speaking life into us. When he got to me, he referenced **finding forgiveness for yourself after the mistake**—reminding me that *there is* **no condemnation** Romans 8:1, (KJV).

Although I couldn't fully grasp that scripture at the time, it did my heart good just to hear him speak life over me. It broke up all the embarrassment and the constant **"it's my fault" running through my mind**. For the first time in a long time, I felt a little lighter, like maybe I didn't have to carry all that blame anymore. I got over the pain, moved on, and picked up where I left off—**single and saved!**

Understanding Salvation Beyond Buildings

I didn't understand the concept of '**God *without* the building**', because all my life I had heard we were not to forsake the assembling of ourselves together Hebrews 10:25, (KJV). If I missed even one Sunday, in my head, I had "forsook everybody and everything." So, I made it my mission to be there every single Sunday for years—no matter which church I attended.

I mean, Sundays belonged to God, right?

The first time I ever pondered anything different was when my Pastor preached a sermon titled, "*Why Do You Come to Church?*" Whew chile—this one opened up the windows of Heaven for me, because I boldly began to ask myself, *Why DO you come to church every Sunday?*

And for the first time in my life, I had to admit... I wasn't coming for Jesus alone.

I was coming because I feared man's opinion if I didn't. I came because that's what they said we were supposed to do. I came to avoid the guilt trips that came with *not* coming.

Lord, I was even living a lie through church attendance—because I didn't even want to be there half the time! Again, I didn't mind going, but let me choose *when* I come—and leave me alone if I decide not to.

That message stuck with me like no other because I realized I wasn't doing it solely from the heart. And one thing I remember hearing throughout life—and adopting as one of my mottos—was: *"If you're not doing something from your heart, don't do it."*

I don't know if that was scripture or just a wise saying, but it became a thorn in my side as I began to wrestle with church attendance.

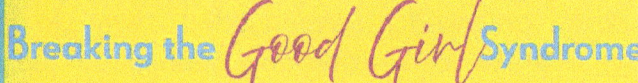

Breaking the *Good Girl* Syndrome

PART 3

THE DIVINE INTERRUPTION

When God Rescues You from the Very Thing That Claimed to Represent Him

CHAPTER 7

The Epiphany That Broke the Chains

Divine Rhema Word and the Deprogram Prayer

By now, I was really starting to question the purpose of the Church—for several reasons. I was tired of seeing the same thing Sunday after Sunday: the saved preaching to the saved, following the same program that was "subject to change by the leading of the Holy Spirit," yet Sunday after Sunday, hardly anything changed.

I also witnessed a homeless man being treated terribly because he was asleep on the back step of the church. He was asked to leave in the worst kind of way, followed by a statement from the Pastor: *"We thank God for protecting the building."* Just before, morning service began.

There was also constant encouragement not to give money to panhandlers, paired with negative remarks about them not working or what they might spend the money on.

The last straw for me came one afternoon after service. We were sitting in the sanctuary talking and laughing when a woman came in asking for financial assistance—and she was refused the help she needed.

Now, I understand to an extent that maybe giving money to people who come in off the street may not always be ideal, as it could deplete church resources. However, I had officially been at this church for six years and had never seen anyone come in like that. One simple act of kindness could have won her to Christ.

One thing for sure—if I'd had it, I surely would have given it to her. This was a major turnoff for me because I've always been a people person, and by now, it looked as though, *"If they don't look like us or aren't a part of us, we ain't got nothing for them."*

I completely disagreed. I thought, *What if that homeless man was an angel?* And *what would Jesus do (W.W.J.D.)* for the panhandler?

I was over judgmental church folk—but what really did it for me came in 2015.

I knew every young person who lost their lives to senseless gun violence in Durham. My heart was so heavy, and I became so angry, wondering, *"What in the world is the church doing?"*

The people in the streets need us, yet we come in here every Sunday, recycling the Word to those already saved. I was so ready to leave the church, but I was afraid—afraid of what people would say and afraid of what God would do. So, I stayed, because I had made a promise, and to leave the church was to leave God.

Time went on, but not much longer after these occurrences,

I was lying across my bed on my back, listening to the Book of Romans on my Bible app. Out of nowhere, I had an *epiphany moment* about my deliverance from crack cocaine!

I said, *Wait a minute—they taught us when I was younger that the only prayer God hears from a sinner is the repentance prayer. If that was true, then how did I get my deliverance from crack cocaine only moments after I had just taken a hit?*

I was higher than Cooter Brown!

I hadn't stepped foot in anyone's church in almost ten years, nor had I asked the Lord for His salvation. It was another moment when I realized that something I had been taught might have been wrong—and if it was, I wanted it out of me. When I realized this, I prayed and asked God to *deprogram me*—to remove anything I had learned that was contrary to His truth. Not only had I experienced this epiphany moment, but I also received a *divine revelation* from Him answering a question I had never even asked—only pondered in my heart.

I had often wondered, *Why was I never able to say or come into agreement with,* "Hello, my name is Tiffany, and I am a *recovering addict*"?

One day, while washing dishes, He began to speak and said, "*'ING' is a form of the present tense, and I have delivered—'ED'—you.*"

I smiled, because I knew exactly what He was answering. And boy, did I want to know this man! Such a sweet and subtle revelation about something I had simply pondered for a while. He was so gentle and kind.

I realized the God who was talking to me was not the God I had known or been taught about. The One speaking to me now seemed so loving and compassionate, while the one I had been taught about was so harsh and scary.

Realizing I Feared God's Punishment, Not Reverenced His heart

At some point, I realized I had pseudo-reverence for Him. I didn't have a reverence for His heart—I was afraid of Him. I was terrified of the punishment He might bring if I didn't get "it" right—fast—before I ended up making hell my home. And in my mind, there were so many "its" to get right. My inability to follow all the rules tormented me internally, and I battled in my mind constantly—even while reading the Word and trying to renew my mind.

It was a never-ending cycle of just can't get it right. And because of it, I didn't just run from the devil—I ran from God.

I can even remember telling God at one point, through pure tears, that I didn't think I was going to make it into Heaven, because no matter how hard I tried to keep the rules, I couldn't. That realization broke my heart on levels I can't even explain.

Here I was, well into my late 30s, giving up on the idea of making Heaven my home.

I read Romans 8:1 (KJV) so many times, but I couldn't grasp it. I lacked the understanding that it referred to willful, unrepentant sin. To me, if I had sinned "yesterday," that meant I was no longer walking after the Spirit—I was walking after the flesh.

If something went wrong in my life, I always assumed it was God's punishment for something I didn't do right. Then there were the times I felt like I was doing everything right but still being punished by God because I hadn't done it perfectly.

This paralyzed me in decision-making. I overthought every move.

I remember receiving a prophetic word that said, "The enemy uses your own heart against you, but the Lord says to tell you—you don't have a bad heart."

I knew that was straight from the Lord because the condition of my heart has always mattered deeply to me. I kept my heart before Him, yet I stayed trapped in my head—always wondering if God was punishing me for some reason or another.

This battle started in childhood and followed me well into adulthood.

Asking for Freedom from False Foundations

I didn't want to be afraid of God anymore. I wanted to know Him in a deeper way—the mysteries I'd always wondered about.

The One who defended the woman caught in the act of adultery. The One who said, *"He who is without sin, let him cast the first stone"* John 8:7, (KJV). The One who said it is love that covers a multitude of sins, I Peter 4:8, (NKJV).

The One who laughs.

The One who, along the way, showed me snippets of love I hadn't experienced yet. The One who said, *"Lay aside every weight"* Hebrews 12:1, KJV). The rescuer. The heart fixer. The mind regulator—without all the heaviness.

I wanted to know *that* God, but I didn't know how to get there. And no one around me seemed to know how either. So, my heart's cry became these private conversations with Him.

I told Him the desires of my heart concerning Him and how I truly aimed to please the Audience of One. I told Him I was sorry for all my sins—particularly my times of fornication. I told Him that no matter how hard I tried not to, I would always give in and then feel the weight of guilt afterward. I told Him I truly didn't want to keep doing that.

I also began to talk to Him about the deep pains within me—how I didn't want to be angry anymore, how I wanted to forgive but didn't know how. I told Him I didn't want to be bitter toward those who had hurt me, nor did I want to hold grudges.

I wanted to be healed—from all the hurts, pains, traumas, and my own negative image of myself. I didn't want to feel like I was walking on pins and needles anymore. I didn't want to live in bondage, nervousness, or anxiety when it came to the things of God.

I didn't want to think the way I thought anymore.

I wanted my mind healed. I wanted to be set free from everything I had been taught about Him up to this point. I wanted to be delivered from the behaviors rooted in fear of Him.

Silently, I was crying out for a **freedom** I knew deep down *had to exist.*

I began asking Him bolder questions, even though I had been taught never to question God. I wanted to laugh again. I wanted to be carefree—not careless or foolish—but free in my mind, body, and soul.

- Because I was sick of church.
- Sick of the know-it-alls.
- Sick of the heaviness and the weight of it all.

I needed answers.

CHAPTER 8

When the Wilderness Is the Rescue

The breakdown, the accident, and the transition to Breath of Life Church

Ever heard the saying, *"Be careful what you pray for?"* Well, I won't go as far as to say that—but I will say this: after you pray for what you want, follow it up with *"Lord, prepare me for how the answer is coming."*

By now, I was over church—because I was being preached *at* from the pulpit. I had seen it happen to several members, and now it was my turn. Around that same time, I desired a change in my career, so I left twenty-five-plus years of administrative work to enter the mental health field as a **Certified Peer Support Specialist**.

This was a huge transition because it required a different kind of discipline, integrity, honesty, and time management—without the structure of a time clock or a supervisor watching over me.

I started full-time and knew I could do it, but in the beginning, it was challenging staying on track with my notes and client visits. This sometimes required me to work on Sundays—and then came the shade from the pulpit.

First, it was, *"You can't serve God and mammon."*

But because I had already witnessed someone else go through it, the guilt didn't hit me right away. My inner response was, *Ain't nobody trying to serve mammon—I'm trying to pay my bills just like you!*

But why was I even defending myself? I hadn't done anything wrong. My job just required more of me. Yet before I could get fully adjusted to this new field, I was already being judged.

Those comments continued to come from the pulpit, and before long, I began to feel guilty for working on Sundays and missing church.

I mean, here I was—six years strong with this ministry—and I could count on both hands how many times I had ever missed church.

About six months into the job, my life started taking hits I didn't see coming. In fact, I didn't even recognize them as hits at first, because they seemed like everyday people problems. But at some point, I remember saying, *What is going on?*—because it was truly one thing after another.

That wasn't even language I used, because I understood the power of words. Calamity after calamity, and you know what I did? I told myself I must have done something wrong and that God was punishing me.

The last hit came when my car completely broke down. I went from a 40-hour workweek to a 6-hour workweek, because peer support required transportation. The company I worked for turned their back on me—as if I hadn't just received an award and a bonus check the week before at our quarterly meeting.

My peers were reassigned to others, and I was left facing another financial struggle. But this one was different—it came with something else.

I began to feel like something was happening to my mind as well.

My comeback wasn't "comebacking."

The resource girl—the one everyone called when they couldn't figure something out, the one who always found a way—was suddenly struggling with her own mental capacity and physical pain as the ache in my lower back worsened.

By August 2017, I knew I was battling some form of depression.

Now, I wasn't one to claim diagnoses lightly. From previous research, I knew many symptoms of depression mirrored the ways people naturally react to stress, so "depression" wasn't something I was quick to accept. But my ability to perform was slipping, and my motivation was nearly gone.

Still, I was moving—pushing through, because I couldn't let my godbaby down after promising to plan her baby shower earlier that year. By God's grace, I completed it, and it was a hit. Right after that came *the accidents* that changed my life—and became the answer to my "deprogram me" prayer from 2015.

During the first week of January 2018, I was in a car accident. Nine days later, a truck ran off the road and hit my home.

There wasn't a soul that could tell me this wasn't God coming for me. And the shade still coming from the pulpit didn't help. The one that pierced my heart—and sent me into a panic attack right there on the pew—was:

> *"You're going through what you're going through because you're not coming to church. Sometimes you have to deal with things by yourself when you don't listen."*

In that moment, it felt like a dagger had hit me in the heart. I gasped for air and burst into uncontrollable tears—so much so that I had to be escorted to the front row for prayer.

Honestly? I didn't want it.
I wanted everyone to get their hands off me.

Resentment and anger started rising, and I just wanted out. But once again, I was too afraid of what kind of punishment might come from God if I left.

By then, I was partially convinced that maybe I *was* going through what I was going through because of my absences. I was confused, because by this time, I had started back attending regularly.

The pain in my body was indescribable, and my mental capacity was rapidly declining. Yet there I was—still being talked about for not coming to church.

As time passed, I began to have massive suicidal thoughts that I couldn't control. I developed insomnia and noticed I was having trouble even leaving the house.

I knew something was happening—but I didn't know what. And I hadn't told a soul, because I was the strong one. The strong one tries to figure it out.

One night, I was awakened out of my sleep by a horrendous pain running up and down my leg—as if someone was cutting me. I screamed and wept, not understanding why this was happening or why now. Things had actually been going well in my new field. I was preparing to launch a clothing closet in honor of my grandmother, for my future transitional home—PMUC.

The thought that hovered in my mind was, *What did I do, Lord?*

At that point, I knew I needed to tell someone. The suicidal thoughts were getting louder, and for a split second, I even caught myself thinking about driving my car off a bridge as that voice in my head pushed me toward it. I called my best friend and told her I was having suicidal thoughts and didn't want to be here anymore.

I also cried out to God and told Him, *"I need a rescue. If You don't come rescue me, I'm not going to make it!"*

That day, I found out just how much of a friend my bestie really was—and just how much she loved me. Within an hour, there was a knock at my door. When I opened it, Lenita LaShonn stepped in proclaiming loudly, **"We tells hell NO!"**

And for the first time in at least two months, I laughed. I needed that.

The thoughts were taking over, and my only prayer at that point was, *"Lord, I just want to think straight."*

Suicide was running through my mind so fast, I didn't have any other thoughts—and that was terrifying.

After that night, I told everyone who needed to know that I was going on a ten-day consecration. My only instructions were: *Don't call me. Don't come by my house.*

All I knew was I needed to hear from God—because something was beating me down, and I didn't like it. Period.

During that time, the Lord instructed me to get rid of all the clothing I had collected for PMUC. I gathered everything, took a photo, and posted it on Facebook tagging three nonprofit organizations I was connected to.

Elder RC responded and told me to call her—so I did, immediately.

When she answered, she said, "What's up, sis?"

I explained what the Lord had told me and described what I was experiencing in my body. The more I talked, the quieter she became. When I finished, she asked if I was still attending the last church she'd seen me at.

I chuckled and said yes, asking why she wanted to know.

Her response stopped me cold:
"Sis, that's where your pain is coming from. It's time to leave there."

Now, wait. I was over my leaders for the shade, but I hadn't planned on leaving. As far as I was concerned, it was just another "church folk" situation—and I had plenty of experience

getting over those. But this wasn't that.

This was God—coming for me.
Answering my prayer by way of the wilderness.

Still, I wasn't convinced. After I hung up, I went into mental turmoil about it, adding to the agony I was already feeling in my body. I was now walking with a cane, bent over, tired, depleted, and scared.

I didn't leave right away, but I did start attending church with my best friend on some Sundays. I was filled with guilt, though, because if the doors of *your* church were open, how dare you be somewhere else—<u>especially without permission</u>!

But the Holy Spirit quickly broke that up.

While I was dancing in the corner at my best friend's church, releasing and getting what I needed, a prophet came up to me and yelled in my ear over the drums:

"God said, stop feeling guilty for being here, getting what you need. You don't go to the eye doctor for your foot! This isn't where you belong—but you're here getting what you need."

It felt like the hammer that began chipping away at all that guilt and heaviness.

I was relieved—relieved that it was okay with God that I was at my best friend's church. I could appreciate the clarity that, even though it wasn't where I belonged, I was still right where I needed to be.

Back to square one, I wondered: *Was I supposed to leave, or was the Evangelist wrong?*

Well, I guess she heard me—because she called to check in.

When I asked where I was supposed to go if I left, she rebuked me:

"See, your problem is you want to know all the steps—all the answers. That's not how God works. When He told Abraham to leave his family, He didn't give him all the instructions. He just said go—and Abraham obeyed. You've got to obey the first instruction."

And she was right.

I don't know why I was questioning it, because things weren't getting any better at the church. I had now been diagnosed with Major Depression, PTSD, Situational Anxiety, and Chronic Back Pain—all while still battling suicidal thoughts.

Some people at church started acting strangely toward me, but because I'd always been the one to take the blame, I thought it was me.

Then one Sunday after service, a young lady I was close to started walking down the aisle toward me. I smiled, ready to greet her with a hug, but she suddenly turned around and walked away.

I froze. *Did that really just happen?*

Before I could finish processing it, another member came up to me and said quietly, "You saw what you saw."

I nodded and said, "Say no more."

I was heartbroken as I walked out. Deep down, I knew—it was time to leave.

But I didn't know *how* to leave. I didn't want anyone saying I left because I was offended.

I began to talk to God about it. I asked Him to give me the words to say and to help me with what I felt toward my leaders, because deep down, I knew they loved their people.

The next service I attended was a revival. While sitting on the pew, I heard the Lord say, *"Praise Me."*

So I got up—in excruciating pain—and slid out from the pews, moving side to side in slow motion because that was all I could do. Pain had consumed my body in a way I can't even describe.

As I praised Him, there was no music, no encouragement, no one joining in—just me being obedient to the Lord.

When I finished and sat down, the revivalist said, *"While the young lady was praising, I heard the Lord say, 'Whom the Son sets free is free indeed'"* John 8:36, (KJV).

And suddenly, the congregation had hallelujahs to offer.

The next day, I realized something—my thoughts were clear.

The suicidal voices were gone.

I stopped dead in my tracks and yelled, *"Thank You, God! Thank You!"*

He freed me from the suicidal thoughts in my obedience to praise Him—and in that same moment, He snatched me out of religion.

Little did I know, that would be my last time attending that church.

Whom the Son sets free is free indeed—that scripture carries deep weight for me because it marked the moment I received my deliverance from the Father.

About a week before that service, I had heard about Breath of Life Church—a safe place where the Pastor truly had a heart for the people. I was told that many had been set free through her obedience to God, so I decided to visit.

I walked in broken—physically, mentally, emotionally, financially, and spiritually. But the moment I entered, I felt peace. The atmosphere was beautiful, and I knew I was in the right place.

After the sermon, there was an altar call. Although I was in an unfamiliar place, I didn't care if the Lord rebuked me in front of the whole congregation—I just wanted to *hear* from Him.

With my eyes closed, tears flowing, and sweat dripping down my face from worship, I stood bent over on my cane at the altar—waiting my turn to receive prayer.

Meeting God as Father, not as Judge

But then it happened—someone came close to my ear and said, *"The Lord said He purposed this for your freedom. He said He's coming to introduce you to the Loving Father, because you never met Him—you were only introduced to the Judge. He also said to call your family by name out of your back,"* and deliverance started immediately.

God wanted to show me who I was in Him, and from that day until this day, He has never said a thing about sin. He never ridiculed me—He just began to tell me who I was in Him, building me up piece by piece.

I knew this was the place for me, and after attending for a few weeks, I joined the ministry. I still didn't quite understand all that was happening, but at some point, I realized this was my *wilderness*—my point of rescue—the very thing I had cried out to God for.

It was a love so sweet and caring, yet I was still angry, disappointed, and disgusted at what I was going through. This disruption had interrupted my entire life. It felt as though I had been dumped on my head and left with a mess to clean up—and that's exactly what I set out to do.

Miss *"do it in my own strength"* began to fight the very One who came to rescue her.

The Father was calling me into a season of *rest*, and that was a language I didn't know how to speak—a level of trust I didn't have yet.

I won't pretend that I immediately came into alignment with God's plans for my life. This wasn't easy at all. I fought Him as if there was a chance of winning—as if there would ever be a *"Tiffany 1, God 0"* moment.

But as I fought, He continued to meet me with a love, compassion, and grace I didn't understand.

All my baggage came with me, which made this journey an uphill battle.

Love and deliverance that didn't scream—it whispered

Months before the accidents, I began to hear **two scriptures** over and over again:

"For My thoughts are not your thoughts, neither are your ways My ways," declares the Lord. "As the heavens are higher than the earth, so are My ways higher than your ways and My thoughts than your thoughts." Isaiah 55:8–9, (NIV)

and

> *"Above all, love each other deeply, because love covers a multitude of sins."* I Peter 4:8, (NIV)

Breath of Life Church looked like *"Love that covers a multitude of sins."* It was truly my safe, healing place. My experience with deliverance there—on day one—was like no other. It was the beginning of my healing and deliverance journey, and I know God strategically placed me there.

When I walked in, I felt peace within, and peace in the environment, even though my body and mind were in turmoil. After that very first session at the altar, I felt so much lighter—and I was off to the races, because it felt *so good* to have some of that weight lifted.

Deliverance is like an onion, and God peeled away each layer—one by one—exposing the things that had interrupted the path He set for me from the beginning of time.

I remember talking to God about wanting to be healed from the trauma and pain of rape. It was the one thing I could barely talk to Him about—let alone anyone else. But God, being omniscient, knew exactly where to start. He went straight to the pain and trauma of domestic violence, touching it first—tenderly, yet with the authority only God could have. I learned early that this journey would be Holy Spirit–led, every step ordered by the Lord. So, I took full advantage of the opportunity and simply showed up—with full expectation for my deliverance.

My journey with Breath of Life Church lasted four years and ended in October 2022.

I walked in as a total stranger—broken, bound, full of resentment, anger, unforgiveness, bitterness, fear, doubt, and disappointment. But God's servants loved me back from a hard place. And for that, I am eternally grateful.

CHAPTER 9

Diagnosing the Root, Not the Fruit

Why Religion Fixes Behavior, but Freedom Heals the Heart

There came a time in my walk when hearing *sin* talked about from the pulpit felt like nails on a chalkboard. And I'm not referring to sin being referenced in its proper scriptural context during a sermon—I mean when it was used as a scare tactic, a tool of guilt, or a means of control by leaders.

I would quietly mutter under my breath, *"Why do they keep talking about sin?"*

They were preaching disproportionately about sin, but the Bible says we're called to preach the Gospel—the Good News of Jesus Christ (Mark 16:15; Romans 1:16). Sure, addressing sin is important—after all, all have sinned (Romans 3:23)—but focusing on sin more than the Good News misses the heart of God's message. The Gospel is about grace, redemption, and the power of Jesus to transform lives (II Corinthians 5:17). But hey, what did little ole me know?

It irritated me so much I wanted to throw my shoe—literally. I didn't even understand why it bothered me so deeply at the time, but on my healing journey, I found out why:

God never intended for man to *teach people about their sin.*

The Word of God says, *"Love covers a multitude of sins"* I Peter 4:8, (KJV). It is only by exalting Jesus that man can and will be delivered.

When you teach *sin*, you cause people to focus on their shortcomings, which drives them to work harder at keeping rules instead of living in Christ.

I experienced this firsthand during my time at Breath of Life Church. Sure, as we called out demons, we discussed the sins that opened the doors—but when someone slipped back into sin, we loved them out of it. Period. Sin wasn't the focus; the love of Christ was. God never spoke to me about sin. He simply lifted my head, straightened my back, and reminded me who I was in Him.

That's what made me want to stop sinning—it wasn't fear, it was love.

It was His love, poured over me again and again.

When you diagnose the fruit and not the root, you're wasting your time. If you really want to kill something, you have to go after it at the root.

So, I had to ask myself: *What is the root of the thing I struggle with?*

One of my struggles was fornication. No matter how many times I tried to stop in my own strength, I couldn't—except when I wasn't in a relationship.

One of the root issues of that struggle was "Daddy Issues"—looking for love in all the wrong places.

But as I allowed God to heal those father wounds, the attention from broken men no longer appealed to me. It became more important to please the heart of God than to satisfy my flesh.

Religion teaches rule-keeping—magnifying sin and diagnosing the fruit of a thing instead of dealing with its root.

For every stumbling block, cycle, sin, or weight in your life, take the time to evaluate and heal the *root* with the leading of the Holy Spirit—and the *fruit of the Spirit* will follow.

I changed my mind completely the day I read this verse:

Galatians 2:19 (MSG) – *What actually took place is this: I tried keeping rules and working my head off to please God, and it didn't work. So I quit being a "law man" so that I could be God's man. Christ's life showed me how, and enabled me to do it. I identified myself completely with Him.*

That was the day I stopped striving to fix my behavior—and started letting God heal my heart.

Setting boundaries without guilt

People-pleasing, the need for man's approval, fear of people's opinions, and constant guilt trips had me out here in these streets without a boundary in sight. But on my healing journey, I realized—not only did I not have any boundaries—I didn't even know *how* to set them.

I had allowed people to do so many things concerning my life, and because I always operated from a place of support, I did *the most*—without even realizing I had become everybody's "do" and "yes" girl.

At first, setting boundaries felt like pulling teeth. I realized just how many people didn't respect me, which made me angry. But even deeper than that, I recognized my own lack of self-respect, because I kept breaking the very boundaries I was trying to set.

BUT GOD!

It was my loving Father who taught me it's okay to set healthy boundaries, tear down unhealthy relationships, and build healthy ones. He knew I was still wrestling with guilt—more concerned about the feelings of others than my own emotional and spiritual well-being.

I'll never forget the day God sent my pastor to tell me, "Stop trying to make your mother feel alright—I've got her, just like I've got you." That moment right there? Another dose of freedom. I'd carried so much guilt about how things changed between my mom and me when God called me into that wilderness season. But when the Author and Finisher of my faith sent that word, all that guilt lifted—I was finally able to let it go. From that moment forward, I started setting boundaries without guilt in every relationship I had.

And I also stopped giving explanations for my movements.

The best part?
It's all from a healed place.

And **God is pleased.**

Honesty as Deliverance:
Learning Not to Counterfeit My Heart

Deliverance will teach you how to be honest—no matter who gets offended—and I say that with a heart full of love. It is never my desire to offend anyone, because the Word tells us not to offend *and* not to be easily offended. But what I've found is this: some people will take issue when you tell them the truth, even when it's spoken with sincere kindness.

God requires us to live in truth, and can I be honest? I absolutely love that God has freed me from false nobility and false humility!

Both are deceptive. Both are rooted in pride, no matter how they show up. They're all about pretending—and pretending requires a mask.

And I, for one, was finally ready to take off every mask.

One of the ways false humility showed up in my life was through self-deprecating humor. I used jokes to downplay my strengths and make fun of my weaknesses—putting myself down while laughing. I didn't realize the real issue underneath was low self-esteem and my ongoing battle with perfectionism.

Then there was my rigid adherence to rule-keeping, which made me focus more on rules than on relationship. Everything was performance-based. I just wanted to please God—and everyone else. That mindset kept me anxious, pretending, and exhausted. When people offended me, I would often retreat into hiding—crying, fuming, then suppressing it all deep down. I'd come back acting like I was okay, letting them right back into my life and close to my heart.

God does call us to forgive and to be kind, but what I didn't know was this: forgiving someone doesn't require reentry into your life.

I was so afraid of being labeled "unforgiving" or "unsaved" that I allowed toxic cycles to repeat. The phrase *"I thought you were saved"* was a tactic the enemy used on me many times. Every time someone said it, I would shrink back—until God freed me from that too.

One evening, during a prayer assignment, the Holy Spirit said clearly: "Do not counterfeit your heart."

Let me explain with two real examples.

The first example was when I had $35 I was planning to sow into a ministry, but I felt this strong pull not to give it—and honestly, I didn't understand why. Still, I obeyed and held onto it. A few days later, God made it clear—through a teaching on the Courts of Heaven. When you give with the wrong heart posture, you release a *testimony* into the Courts of Heaven that can give the enemy legal rights into your finances.

That revelation shook me. Giving is good—but if your heart posture or your motive is even a little off, it can open doors in the spirit you never intended to open. I remember sitting there, thinking, *Wow...God isn't just concerned about the act of giving—He's concerned about the why and the how behind it.* And in that moment, He gave me a fresh understanding:

obedience isn't just about what you do—it's about the condition of your heart when you do it. The second situation involved preparing goodie bags for a group of people who had recently been baptized. Among them was a young woman who had offended me several times over the years. Despite that, I genuinely loved her and was happy about her new life in Christ, so I began making her bag like everyone else's.

But before I could finish, she offended me again. It triggered what hadn't yet been fully healed.

I decided to forgive her and walk that forgiveness out, but I still wrestled—*Should I give her the bag or not?*

At first, I told myself, *Give her the bag, Tiffany. Don't let anyone change your heart posture.*

But deep down, I had to ask:
Am I really giving this from a pure heart? Or am I just worried people will think I'm bitter if I don't—especially if they found out I had given everyone else who was baptized a bag?

That was the real issue.

In honesty, my heart toward her wasn't in the right place, and I realized I was more concerned about man's opinion than God's instruction. So I didn't give her the bag.

If I had, I would've been counterfeiting my heart—and giving the enemy another open door.

Sounds just like the Word, doesn't it?

II Corinthians 9:7 (NIV) – *Each of you should give what you have decided in your heart to give, not reluctantly or under compulsion, for God loves a cheerful giver.*

I didn't have to worry about what people would think. If someone accused me of holding a grudge, I could raise my shield of faith to block those fiery darts—because I was walking in obedience.

Oh, if we would just obey the Word!

God's wisdom and instruction are perfect—and always purposeful. I did eventually sow that $35 into the ministry, but it was after my heart posture was corrected.

This is not an excuse *not* to give—it's a reminder, a deeper revelation of *how* and *why* you give.

Check your heart.

Could it be that the reason many of us never see "pressed down, shaken together, and running over" (Luke 6:38, KJV) is because we've been giving grudgingly, out of obligation, or—worse—with the wrong motive or heart posture? Could it be that the enemy is bringing accusations against us in those very areas—and because we haven't repented, the Father, being just, must allow the enemy legal access?

God is strategic, just, and fair—but He's not a liar. He will never break His own law just to protect us from the consequences of disobedience.

Breaking the *Good Girl* Syndrome

PART 4

THE BECOMING

**Stepping Into the Identity
I Was Always Meant to Carry**

CHAPTER 10

He Called Me by Name

The Names He Gave Me: Kingdom Financier, Watchman, Arsenal, and more

If God never revealed another thing about who I am in Him, I promise you—I already have enough revelation to truly *occupy until He comes.*

What I found to be true is this: the enemy isn't threatened by your church attendance, your shout, your dance, your worship, or even your preaching. He's threatened by one thing—you knowing who you are in Christ.

Religion told me everything I was *not,* but freedom revealed who I am.

During my healing process, God changed my name. I had to learn how to come out of agreement with everything contrary to what He said about me. I began to identify every lie of the enemy and one by one—renounced, denounced, dismantled, and severed every tie I had made with the kingdom of darkness.

I have nothing to do with Satan, and he has nothing to do with me. And the best part? Every name God gave me resonated deeply—it was who I had been all along.

For example, I've always loved shows like *Law and Order*, *Murder She Wrote*, *Matlock*, and *Criminal Minds*. That fascination spoke directly to my "Prophetic Lawyer Girl" identity and the Esther and Deborah anointings over my life.

There's something inside of you right now that might cause agitation or irritation, and you don't even know why. For me, it was anytime someone discredited prayer—especially during social media debates about justice and faith. When people would say, *"We need to do more than pray, because Faith without works is dead,"* I'd be yelling at my phone, *"PRAYER IS A WORK!"*

I would think of all the mothers who *tarried at the altar* until breakthrough came—dripping with sweat and tears for souls. I'd be fired up defending prayer online, yet I didn't even have a prayer life myself at the time!

Now I know why those comments bothered me so much. God later revealed I have the gift of intercession. When He called me His Prophetic Intercessor, He also announced that *all of hell would obey my voice.*

Long before that revelation, He had already called me His Kingdom Sniper and Watchman, which explained the agitation. A Kingdom Sniper—in spiritual context—is a skilled intercessor, someone with keen spiritual insight and strategic prayer precision.

A Watchman is one positioned for vigilance, assigned to warn, intercede, and protect.

Do you see where this is going?

How could I stay bent over after that? How could I *not* rise with new confidence? How could this revelation *not* draw me closer to Him? I've been dancing with Him all my life—following His subtle cues, not even knowing it.

I call Him the "Dot Connector."

Developing a relationship with Jesus Christ has kept me in awe, constantly amazed as He helps me understand my thoughts, habits, and even childhood tendencies through the lens of divine purpose.

I'm far from perfect and have done plenty wrong—but there's always been a standard I've lived by:

The Golden Rule—to treat others the way I want to be treated. That's when God gave me another name: Standard Bearer.

It happened so naturally. One day, while at home, I was thinking out loud:

"Why do I always have to be the bigger person? Why can't I do to people what they do to me and not feel guilty? Why am I always the one hurt and crying?"

I wasn't even talking to God, just pouting.

That following Sunday, as I was walking past my Pastor on the way to pre-service prayer, she chuckled and said,

"God said, because you are the Standard Bearer."

I kept walking, no explanation needed. I knew exactly what God was answering. I might have rolled my eyes a little as she laughed—but she was right. He calls me so much more, and I have work to do on this earth.

I've promised myself I will leave this world *empty*—having poured out everything He placed inside of me.

Hello, my name is Tiffany— the Repairer of the Breach, a Frontliner, a Wailing Woman, an Arsenal for the Kingdom, a Business Coach, a Creative, a Master Photographer, the Credit Negotiator, a Kingdom Financier, a Published Author, a Deliverance Minister, a Weapon of Mass Destruction, a Quartermaster, and a Generational Curse Breaker—anointed with the Esther, Deborah and Breaker's Anointing, who absolutely gets on hell's nerves, says the Lord.

Seeing Myself Through His Eyes for the First Time

Learning to see myself through the Freedom-framed lens of Christ came with a cost—but it also came with the great reward of meeting new versions of myself and a deeper relationship with Abba Father.

I'm just getting started on exploring this new me, watching myself grow and evolve.

Seven years into my healing journey has not been easy. I've cried more in these seven years than I probably have in my entire life. God came to break me, but it was never to hurt or punish me—it was to help me see myself as He sees me:

- **fearfully and wonderfully made**
- **full of power and authority.**

He wanted me to stop comparing myself to others and finally recognize that I am His masterpiece.

He broke me so I could glorify Him by helping others step into this same freedom and deliverance.

Oh, what a mighty God I serve!

I've lost people—and I'm still losing people—and the grief is real.

But there is nothing more rewarding than being able to thank God for the *affliction* and mean it when I say:

"Though You slay me, yet will I trust You." Job 13:15, (KJV)

I've endured disrespect, dishonor, mishandling, and mistreatment for being the chosen one—but I've learned to trust God wholeheartedly, to just **be**, and to ignore anyone who calls me anything other than **Tiffany**.

I look just like my Father—made in His image, given a name that means "*Divine Revelation of God, Manifestation of God, and the Appearance of God.*"

I will not answer to anything else.

The **people-pleaser** has left the building.

No matter how hard the journey has been, I still aim to please the **Audience of One**, because I understand that:

"The sufferings of this present time are not worthy to be compared with the glory which shall be revealed in us." Romans 8:18, (KJV)

Authority that Comes from Love—Not Legalism

At the end of my season at Breath of Life Church, there was another shift—God called me into the Secret Place with Him alone. He invited me to sit at His feet, to reset my thoughts about punishment, and to rebuild my foundation.

He called me out of the building—the very place I once thought qualified me as "saved."

I've been in this secret place for three years now, and that first year was *hard*. I didn't know how to function outside of "doing."

On my first Sunday out of the church building, at 10:00 a.m. sharp (service time), I grabbed my Bible and tried to "have church." And I could feel Holy Spirit whispering behind me: "No… and whoa."

That was full-blown legalism in action—ready to *do* something—when God was about to teach me how to simply be.

I understood the concept, but I hadn't yet lived it. Sitting still was foreign to me. But God slowly chipped away at my striving, teaching me to stand in the authority that comes not from works—but from Love.

- I don't have to perform for it.
- I don't have to buy it.
- I don't have to pretend for it.
- And I certainly don't have to be perfect to receive it.

The perfectionism I struggled with, born from legalism, was my biggest Goliath. But by the grace of God—I have **slayed that giant**. Now I live in the freedom of knowing that **God loves me**, even in my flaws, mess-ups, and "can't get rights."

He's taught me to **trust Him**; even with my missteps, because He is able to **order my steps**.

And **I'm crystal clear on this**:

To go back to that old, rule-keeping, peer-pleasing religion would mean abandoning everything personal and free about my relationship with God.

> *"I refuse to do that, to repudiate God's grace. If a living relationship with God could come by rule-keeping, then Christ died unnecessarily."*
> — Galatians 2:21 (MSG)

CHAPTER 11

Real, Raw, and Redeemed

No More Masks, No More Spiritual Gymnastics

"Indeed, I have been crucified with Christ. My ego is no longer central. It is no longer important that I appear righteous before you or have your good opinion, and I am no longer driven to impress God. Christ lives in me. The life you see me living is not mine, but it is lived by faith in the Son of God, who loved me and gave Himself for me. I am not going to go back on that."

— Galatians 2:20 (MSG)

That scripture says it all for me—in this season and forevermore. Deliverance didn't stop when I left Breath of Life. It continued in the presence of the Lord, and soon after, I was introduced to my **crushing season**.

I realized that the **root of the mask** I wore was my ego—trying to save my own reputation, defend myself, control how others perceived me, and impress God through works. But in the crushing, I came to understand that none of that mattered.

I began to relate to Apostle Paul when he spoke of being *"crushed and overwhelmed beyond his ability to endure,"* but as a result, he *"stopped relying on himself and learned to rely only on God."* II Corinthians 1:8–9, (NLT).

That's exactly what God has done—and still does—every single day for me. I stopped trying to prove a point and came into alignment with what God wanted to birth: the intercessor and the prophet in me. And I have no time to waste on mediocrity.

While at Breath of Life , I was taught that deliverance doesn't end at the altar. You must maintain it—protect it at all costs. I didn't know what that would look like once I returned to the familiar, but one thing was certain: after all the work I'd done, I refused to go backward.

- **I will not wear the mask again.**
- **I will not shrink myself to fill the voids others refuse to face.**
- **I will not perform spiritual gymnastics to make people comfortable.**
- **It's too heavy.**

Not only did the behaviors of others have to go—but so did my own self-sabotaging habits: comparison, self-condemnation, doubt, guilt, people-pleasing, overthinking, pretense, and feeling overlooked.

God sees me—and He's made that clear over and over again. He wants to use me as His vessel, and I've given Him full permission. To get to the authentic me I desired, I had to draw closer to Him—surrender, submit, relinquish control, and align with His way, His will, His order, and His timing.

Deliverance in a church setting is beautiful. Deliverance with man is valuable. But true deliverance comes from *sitting in the presence of the Father*—allowing Him to be the Potter and choosing to be the clay, willing to get back on the wheel as many times as needed.

Setting Boundaries, Saying No, and Loving from Truth

When I first started setting boundaries, I had it all wrong. I thought boundaries were a way to make people treat me differently—but I quickly learned that boundaries aren't about controlling others. They're about **controlling what you allow** and what you're willing to accept.

Boundaries helped me categorize people—some belong in close proximity, others at the perimeter—and my—Golden Rule (Matthew 7:12)—became the measuring stick. God told me early in my journey that some blessings wouldn't come until my **"No" got stronger**.

At first, my "No" came from anger and frustration—it wasn't pure. Those **"false no's"** didn't last. So, I did a hard reset and prayed, asking God to help me say "No" from a place of truth, not trauma.

One day while talking with my personal trainer, I admitted my struggle with saying no and expressing how I really felt. She looked me straight in the face and said:

"How are you going to be an intercessor and not tell the truth? How are you going to be a lying intercessor—lying to yourself by not being honest with others?"

Can you say *ten-pound weight to the face?*

She was loud, so all I heard echoing in my spirit was **"LIAR!"**—and I couldn't even be mad. She was right.

From that day forward, I started praying for help to express myself better—to actually say **"No"** when I meant it—and to be okay with whatever people thought about it. Honestly, it stung to see how many didn't honor or respect my boundaries. But there were no hard feelings—just a big eye-opener. I simply backed away—because I believe people know exactly what they're doing. And at this point in life, I'm not teaching grown folks how to respect boundaries or my prerogative to say **"No."**

I've learned that familiarity really does breed contempt.

Letting Go of Guilt as a Lifestyle

The Word makes it clear that the enemy's only job is to steal, kill, and destroy, John 10:10, (KJV). And he works *24/7*, using the same tactics—because he has no new tricks. But I've learned to work **25/8** with the guidance of the Holy Spirit. So when the enemy tries to lay a guilt trip on me, I simply ignore him—and the guilt.

- **It's not my portion.**
- **It's not my lifestyle.**
- **I deny access to it.**

I'm learning to live a life that welcomes the convictions of Christ but slams the door shut on condemnation and guilt.

"Resist the devil, and he will flee from you." James 4:7, (KJV)

That's non-negotiable.
Nothing else to talk about.

CHAPTER 12

Healing Isn't Always Pretty, But It's Worth It

Mental Battles, Financial Struggles, and Wrestling with Disappointment

I didn't just suffer mental health battles as God was snatching me from religion to freedom during my 2018 spiritual transition—it happened again in 2022, during my second spiritual transition, when He called me out of the building. The mental health challenges I suffered in 2018 turned out to be a walk in the park compared to the mental battles I endured throughout my healing journey. I can recall attending a conference with my mother in February 2018, and before the conference started, my mother and I went up to the room of the guest speaker.

As we got off the elevator, we heard Holy Ghost–fire prayers coming from her room. When we entered, we saw her and her armor-bearer praying together, doing all this prophetic movement, and when she turned around and saw me, she began to motion as if she was hurling something at me—one hand at a time—praying in tongues. At one point, I heard her say, "light affliction," as she continued to do spiritual warfare and prophesy to me. I got stuck at "light affliction," with an "I beg to differ" attitude sitting on me. What do you mean, *light* affliction? Listen, I was offended, because she couldn't be referencing everything I had been going through as "light"—in my mind, it was the worst thing I had ever experienced. However, by the end of October 2022, I had determined she was right, LOL.

A few months after joining Breath of Life Church, God told me it was my healing place. A few months later, during a pastoral celebration, the guest speaker gave a prophetic word to my leader that Breath of Life was a healing hub, and that the Lord said He was going to cycle people in to get their healing and then send them out to where they were meant to be. His word confirmed the word the Lord had given me, and I thought that was the most beautiful thing—a place for people to safely heal, endorsed by God!

During my next devotion time, I said to the Lord, *You know me, so when it's time for me to leave, don't let me get stuck in lethal loyalty and miss it.* I knew myself well enough to know there was a possibility I might not want to leave, especially after all the love I had received in the few months I had been there.

Sure enough, I missed it—so Daddy had to come snatch me out of there too, and because I thought it was the enemy, I fought ten toes down through spiritual warfare, only to realize once again there was not a win in sight. It started a few weeks before I was snatched. As soon as I would get out of bed to prepare for church, an unusual anxiety would come upon me. The first few times I chalked it up as nothing. Simultaneously, during this time I was learning about angels and learned that when you are experiencing strong mental attacks, you ask the Lord to send the angel of hope.

The following Sunday, I got out of bed to get ready for church—and the moment I did, this crushing anxiety hit my chest. I even backed away from my dresser like it was somehow causing it. I pressed on, muttering, *"Lord, what is this?"* By the time I got to the church, my anxiety was through the roof—like 10 to the tenth power. But as praise and worship started, I threw my hands in the air and told God, *"I don't know what's happening, but You are still worthy of all my praise. I will worship*

You through this." I remembered the angel of hope—and I started praying, asking the Lord to send that angel to help me.

Y'all, within seconds of me calling for the angel of hope, something flew past and *high-fived* my right hand! Instantly, the anxiety lifted right out of my chest. Baby, when I tell you I started singing and praising God from a whole different place—whew! First of all... did something just *high-five* me? Did I just have my first real angel encounter? Wait a minute—did anxiety really just flee after something high-fived me? Oh me, oh my... the joy of the Lord really *is* my strength! God is so awesome and so much bigger than the mental battles and struggles we go through. I'm not here to minimize it, but I am learning to exalt Him above anything that tries to exalt itself against the knowledge of God. Mental battle: defeated!

At the end of 2020, the Lord told me to sit before Him and tell Him everything I was disappointed in Him about—and if I'm honest, I didn't want to do it. For the first time in at least three years, I was in a happy place mentally. I knew following this instruction was going to have me barreled over in tears and mad. But then He said, *Do it now before the new year comes in*. With about a week left in 2020, I obeyed. After sharing the word of the Lord with my Pastor, she told me, *God is about to bring another level of freedom to you*. Yes—let me get that, please! What started out meek and mild turned into a violent rage, and before I knew it, I was yelling at God, giving Him the business. The upset in my finances in 2018 wasn't the first time I struggled financially—it was just the worst one yet.

There were times people had gotten over on me and didn't pay what they owed—and I'm not talking about average folks; I mean agencies I worked for and landlords who kept my deposits—little hits to my finances throughout my life. I was a giver and a tither, and I just didn't understand why I was always dealing with these injustices in my finances. Prayer was always my answer to everything—again, long before God revealed I had the gift of intercession—but it just seemed like God would never come to my rescue. What I didn't know was that the enemy had legal rights to my finances. I had never heard about legal rights or the Courts of Heaven, but God brought the Courts of Heaven across my path years before He snatched me out of religion. I was intrigued but wondered why we weren't being taught these things, so I left it on the shelf.

It wasn't until the end of 2017, as my finances were being hit again, that I connected the dots. I remember being so angry that I grabbed the footboard of my bed by the rails and started slamming it into the floor, yelling, *"Why does this keep happening to me?"* When the bed hit the floor the last time, it was as if the Lord Himself rewound my mind back to the YouTube video He had shown me about the Courts of Heaven. I paused and pondered, *"Lord, is this what this is? Is there a cycle in my finances?"* The Lord had to introduce me to the Courts of Heaven to help me understand why my finances were staggered and stuck.

The enemy had legal rights into my finances, so for **years** I suffered in a cycle: doing well → abrupt job loss → getting behind → tax-time catch up and pay up → regain employment → doing well → abrupt job loss → getting behind → tax-time catch up and pay up → regain employment. Let me run it by you one more time: doing well → abrupt job loss → getting behind → tax-time catch up and pay up → regain employment. Not to mention, I'm also called to the world of finance—which makes it a constant battle, because you often receive your hardest hits in the areas you're called to or have a solution for. I am a Kingdom Financier, period—a lender and not a borrower!

When the Lord gave me the instruction to tell Him about my disappointments, I thought it was all about my finances—until the real thing He was after surfaced: the hurt and pain from the biggest family attack I suffered in 2012 regarding my second granddaughter. That's what took me into that violent rage I mentioned earlier. It happened out of the blue—so unexpectedly. I went from my financial disappointments into this: *And You let them run my name all up and through this family, telling lies on me, and didn't do nothing! All I've ever done was treat people the way I wanted to be treated—and You didn't defend my name! All I've ever done was aim to please You—and You did nothing! They tore up relationships…* Whew, chile—by now I was in full-blown rage, going in on the Father.

I started out in one position, but by the time I finished, I was barreled over in fetal position on the floor—finally releasing hurt, pain, and trauma I had held for eight years. During those eight long years, I had suppressed the pain of the lies, the pain of those who believed them, the pain of who initiated it all, and the trauma of trying to defend myself from so much coming at me so fast. My Pastor was indeed correct—because the weight and burden lifted off me and opened the next level of freedom in my relationship with Abba Father! There was a sense of peace after that, as well as a *"be well, daughter"* from the Father who already knows. He cares for me. I Peter 5:7, (KJV)

He Thanked Me for Loving Him Since I was a Child

At Breath of Life, during the Utterance Retreat,[4] I was introduced to soaking—intentionally quieting your mind and heart to rest in God's presence to receive His grace, strength, and revelation. I loved this because it allowed me to free my mind from the cares of the day and receive the word of the Lord. After my first group experience, I decided to try it at home. Full

---

[4] The Retreat Name has been changed to protect the integrity of the work of the Lord that is being completed through the vessels that carry out that assignment.

of zeal about my new healing place and all things deliverance, I got my pen, notebook, and blanket to lay prostrate before the Lord. After a little while, the Lord began to speak, so I grabbed my pen and wrote. I was like a big kid in a candy store when I would hear the Lord—but on this day, something very special happened—both painful and freeing.

The Lord spoke a lot that day, and as He came to the end, He said to me, "And thank you for always loving Me, even as a little girl." I started yelling, screaming, hollering, kicking the floor, and crying—because it was as if He took a pin and popped this balloon of pressure I had carried for years. So many had insinuated I didn't love Him, using the scripture, *"If you love Me, keep My commandments."* I have loved Jesus since the age of six—working overtime to show Him—but on this day He let me know He saw me the entire time. That was the first hit to the onion layered with so much pain. Deliverance is like an onion—peeled layer by layer to eliminate deep pain. My Father has always seen me!

Why Waiting Well Matters

"But they that wait upon the LORD shall renew their strength; they shall mount up with wings as eagles; they shall run, and not be weary; and they shall walk, and not faint."
(Isaiah 40:31, KJV)

What do you do when you don't know how to wait—and no one has taught you that there is an art to waiting? We hear it all the time—Isaiah 40:31—*if you wait upon the Lord, your strength shall be renewed, and you shall mount up with wings as eagles*. While this is true, I often found myself still on the floor—wishing, hoping, praying, and crying—because guess what? I didn't know how to wait, much less how to wait well. But let me tell you why waiting well matters.

Waiting well builds character, strength, trust, and wisdom. To wait well means to occupy—doing whatever God tells you to do in the season you're in. For some, waiting well may be resting as He instructs—spending more time with Him, clearing your plate of the unnecessary "to-do" list, and learning how to just be. For others, waiting well may look like building your financial capacity by cleaning up your finances and taking a few financial literacy courses. Whatever it is, put your hands to the plow of obedience.

Waiting well also looks like working on additional areas of your life that align with the will of God. Your instructions may lie within your finances, but your health is equally important—so steward that area too. Eat like the royal priesthood and holy nation that you are while building better habits. Work out to present your body a living sacrifice—which is your reasonable service Romans 12:1, (KJV).

The worst thing to do while waiting is nothing—right next to murmuring, complaining, and being disobedient—because it only intensifies the struggle and delays the blessing. The most well-known example is the children of Israel and their forty-year journey from Egypt to Canaan, a result of disobedience, wandering, and complaining. Various Bible scholars have estimated that, based on method of travel, the trip could have taken about ten–eleven days in their time—or roughly nineteen hours with modern transportation.

Nowhere—past or present—should it have taken forty years, and this was a people who saw an entire sea parted for them.

Listen, beloved, we are choosing:

- **to wait well.**
- **Renew your mind in the waiting.**
- **Thank Him in advance in the waiting.**
- **Worship Him in the waiting.**
- **And don't you dare faint.**
  Galatians 6:9, (KJV)

"Resist the devil, and he will flee from you."
James 4:7, (KJV)

"...We were crushed and overwhelmed beyond our ability to endure... But as a result, we stopped relying on ourselves and learned to rely only on God..." II Corinthians 1:8–9, (NLT)
"...Casting all your care upon Him; for He careth for you."
I Peter 5:7, (KJV)

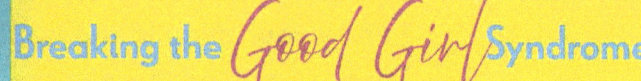

Breaking the *Good Girl* Syndrome

PART 5

THE FREEDOM COMMISSION

An Invitation to Everyone
Who's Ready to Come Out

CHAPTER 13

Spirit and Truth Over Religion and Pretense

Worship Beyond Performance

Prior to being transitioned to Breath of Life Church, worship was just the song that came after praise in the "Praise and Worship" segment of the church program. I closed my eyes and sang my heart out as loud as I could and, although I was very sincere, it was a surface-level performance—accomplishing a task to get through that part of the service. My lack of understanding of what worship truly is caused me to enter into it wrong, and because of my transactional theology, at some point my private worship became a transaction for me.

I often heard people say, "Everything you need is in worship," so I would approach private worship from the perspective of, *"Worship—and while I'm in there, God is going to answer everything right in that moment."* When He didn't, disappointment set in and my immediate thought was, *I didn't do something right.*

At times I thought I had to worship hard and long in exchange for what I wanted from God. It wasn't about material things—I knew His hand all too well. It was more about His face and hearing His voice on matters of my heart. At Breath of Life , I learned we worship God for who He is, period. It's not the time for a petition, not the time to problem-dump, and not the time to expect a thing from Him. It's the time we take to love on Him, adore Him, magnify and exalt Him just because of who He is—the majestic, Almighty, one and only righteous, true, living, holy God—this and so much more.

The first time I approached worship from this new perspective, I felt a gravitational pull downward into a position of bowing. I didn't want to interrupt it, but because I didn't know what it was, there was a little resistance—but only for a moment. Then I relinquished control, and the next thing I knew, I was on the floor on my knees in a full bow. I learned a few years later, while studying the gift of intercession, that when God's glory enters the room, you will more than likely find intercessors bowing. How cool is that?

Today, when I prepare to worship, I go without an agenda—first repenting, then telling Him how matchless He is, then sitting to listen to His heart. As I continue to grow in His wisdom from glory to glory, it is my desire to have a worship encounter where my spirit meets His Spirit totally, because the flesh holds no good thing. *"But the hour cometh, and now is, when the true worshipers shall worship the Father in spirit and in truth; for the Father seeketh such to worship Him."* John 4:23, (CSB)

God Can't Heal Who You Pretend to Be

Who are you? Do you offer yourself to God from a naked and unashamed place? Are you real with Him? Or do you approach Him as I did—masked, hiding from the very One who created you? Do you run *from* Him when guilt rides you, or do you run *to* Him so He can embrace you when you fall short of His glory? I found Him to be just that kind of God—not waiting to punish me with every wrong move, but standing with arms wide open, ready to embrace me.

I discovered on this journey that the worst person you can lie to is *yourself,* because beloved, God already knows you better than you know you. Walking in pretense is heavy and requires effort. I felt like I was constantly walking on pins and needles—smiling when I wanted to cry. While we all have days like that, it had become a *way of life* for me. I even remember my ex-husband calling me the "Great Pretender." As much as it offended me, he was right—filled with so much hurt yet pretending to be okay with everyone who caused it.

BUT GOD! One of the first scriptures I received in my healing journey was Hebrews 12:1, which tells us to *lay aside every weight* (KJV). The weight I carried was so heavy, and I didn't know how to release it. I didn't even know **what** it was—and as I looked around at everyone in my environment, they looked heavy too, with the solemn faces I didn't want. God, with His loving Self, came for me at the tender age of 46 to deliver me, and I will always honor, serve, love, and walk with Him. He is one awesome and amazing Daddy! From *God*, to *Father*, to *Daddy*—now that's a relationship. I tell Him everything; and although He knows all, it matters that *we* acknowledge to Him what He already sees.

You must worship Him in spirit and truth, because He cannot heal who you pretend to be—and He's waiting to do for you *exceedingly abundantly above all that you can ask or think* Ephesians 3:20, (KJV). Now I can mount up, and as I continue on my healing journey, I open myself even more to the Father so our relationship may be cultivated as I choose every day to be the clay that the Master Potter molds and shapes into His desired result.

Your Truth is Your Starting Point— Not Your Disqualification

Where are you in *working out your own salvation with fear and trembling* Philippians 2:12, (KJV)? Can I tell you that your truth is your starting point—and whatever that truth may be, it does not disqualify you.

At the end of the **Utterance Retreat** I attended in 2018, the floor was opened for remarks. One young lady stood up and said she had never felt so free and safe in church to talk about her struggles within her sexuality without feeling judged. Overseer stood and told us that when God called her to pastor, He told her He was sending her out to tear down religion—that He never intended for man to *teach people about their sin*. He instructed her **not** to touch their sin, but to **love** them and let Him handle the sin, because *"love covers a multitude of sins"* I Peter 4:8, (KJV).

Remember my "nails on the chalkboard" moments—one of them was "preaching sin." In that moment, I proclaimed within myself, I knew it! Her mentioning the same scripture I'd been hearing in my spirit months before God snatched me out of religion sealed it.

By then, tears were rolling down my face—God had connected more dots. Most importantly, no matter how many times I was made to feel unworthy, or how many times I messed up and felt unworthy, His revelation assured me that I am connected to Him. I didn't know it then, but in 2024 God revealed I carry the same mandate. My transition to Breath of Life wasn't just about my healing—it was about my assignment. Since leaving, He has revealed that I am also called to, in His words, utterly destroy religion—and I gladly accept the charge.

Will you allow me to start with **you?**
Are you ready for your **freedom in Christ?**

Let's Choose Your Starting Point

Oftentimes, when it comes to forgiveness, we don't consider that we must forgive ourselves. While forgiving others can be challenging, I found that forgiving myself was the biggest challenge. **Forgive yourself.** If this is you, pray the following prayer over yourself.

PRAYER OF FORGIVENESS

Father,
I make a decision to trust you in my process to freedom,
healing and deliverance.
I ask you to meet me at my current level of trust
to guide my way and order my steps.

I'm deciding to surrender my will to your will so that I may experience the fullness of your freedom and love.

*I surrender to you now, every altered version of myself that formed as a result of hurt, pain and trauma and I come into agreement with who you
say I am,
as we walk this journey together.*

*I forgive myself for all the things I didn't know.
I forgive myself for
people-pleasing.*

*I forgive myself for my inability to say no.
I forgive myself for not setting boundaries and I forgive myself for not loving myself.*

*Teach me your ways so that I may live my life according to your will, your way, your order, and your timing,
in Jesus' name
-Amen*

If you have found yourself in a space where everything is crashing down around you, or it feels like you take one step forward and get knocked back five, allow me to pray the following prayer over you—and feel free to pray it over yourself.

PRAYER FOR BREAKTHROUGH

Father, You are the Lord of breakthroughs, and I come boldly to Your throne on behalf of this vessel of use, who has chosen to say yes to the freedom of Christ and embark upon this journey of healing and deliverance.

I thank You that You are a very present help who will show up for them. Father, as they take this journey, I call upon Jehovah Rapha, the Lord who heals, to heal their mind, body, and soul.

Father, according to Your Word (Job 22:28), we shall decree a thing, and it shall be established. Therefore, I decree obedience to every instruction that prepares them for deliverance and the fulfillment of God's promises, even when they don't understand.
I decree that You strengthen them as they work out their own soul salvation and move from glory to glory to become more like You, and may they keep their hearts repentant before You.

I decree that overthinking, torment, self-condemnation, shame, guilt, people-pleasing, performance, comparison, doubt, fear, perfectionism, and religious rule-keeping shall not be their portion. I decree that when they find themselves battle-weary, weak, and faced with adversity that seems too hard to bear, they shall call upon the name of the Lord, and You will answer.

I decree that they cast out every negative thought that exalts itself above who they know You to be and simply know they can do all things through Christ who strengthens them, because they are more than conquerors, and greater is He who is in them than he who is in the world.

Father, according to III John 1:2, You wish above all things that they prosper and be in good health, even as their souls prosper. So I decree that as their souls prosper, every area of their lives shall prosper. I decree that they shall know that rest is a gift from You and that it's okay to unplug from the masses to plug into Your presence.

I decree that the blessings of the Lord make them rich and add no sorrow.
I pray that they will know Your voice and seek Your face.
I decree the freedom to live and experience the fullness of Your love.

According to I Corinthians 12:7 and Romans 12:6-8 may every dormant spiritual and natural gift within this believer rise to the occasion. I break the poverty mindset that causes them to settle for mediocrity and decree they are lenders and have no need to borrow.

I decree you spread your protection from the evil one over them and I call forth failure to every plan of the enemy. I cancel the assignments of principalities, powers, spiritual wickedness in high places and the rulers of darkness of this world. I break the principality of delay off their life and unleash Amos 9:13 like a whirlwind, one blessing fast on the heel of another. I command the enemy to bow and accept his defeat concerning this one in Jesus' Name.

Thank You for deliverance from all evil, the resurrection of every gift, and death by fire to every plan of the enemy. You are indeed matchless, and I am forever grateful for Your gentleness, kindness, patience, and long-suffering. You are the Author and Finisher of our faith, and I decree that the good work You have begun in Your servant shall be performed until the day of Jesus Christ's return. I seal this prayer with the body and blood of Jesus Christ, and I say it is so and shall not be otherwise, in Jesus' Name. Amen!

We all have our reasons for drifting away from God, because let me be clear—He never leaves us. But guess what? You're still here, still breathing, so whatever the reason, it doesn't even matter. If you've strayed from the faith, I'm speaking to you as an Ambassador of Christ: come back to God and be reconciled. He's waiting for you, arms wide open, ready to welcome you home.

The Bible verse II Corinthians 5:18-20 (NIV) reads: "All this is from God, who reconciled us to himself through Christ and gave us the ministry of reconciliation: that God was reconciling the world to himself in Christ, not counting people's sins against them. And he has committed to us the message of reconciliation. We are therefore Christ's ambassadors, as though God were making his appeal through us. We implore you on Christ's behalf: Be reconciled to God."

PRAYER of RECONCILIATION

Father,
It's your daughter/son, [(insert your name)].
I come to You with a repentant heart, asking for forgiveness. Forgive me for my sins and for turning away from You. I thank You for not counting my sin against me, and I ask to be reconciled back to You. It is my desire to experience Your freedom through relationship, as I walk this journey with You in total surrender. In Jesus' Name, Amen.

If you aren't sure that you've ever accepted Jesus as your Lord and Savior, or if you have not yet accepted Him, take it from someone who has experienced both the Judge and the Loving Father—He is a dope God!

You don't have to be afraid of Him, you don't have to worry about being perfect, and you don't have to worry about Him ever leaving you. He will walk with you until the very end.

I want you to, in your own private time, read the following scripture that has been personalized for YOU!

Then pray the simple prayer below over yourself:

Romans 10:9-10 (ESV) ~ "because, if_I confess with_My mouth that Jesus is Lord and believe in My heart that God raised him from the dead, _I will be saved.
For with the heart _I believe and _I am justified, and with the mouth
_I confess and_I am saved."

PRAYER of SALVATION:

Father,
Thank you for your perfect plan of Salvation.

Thank you for giving your son as a sacrifice so that I would not perish and Jesus,

I thank you for being about your Father's business and accepting the assignment just for me.

I confess with my mouth that Jesus is Lord and believe in my heart that you raised Him from the dead.

Not only do I ask you to be my Savior but I give you full permission to be Lord over my life,
In Jesus' name,
Amen.

Beloved, I welcome you into the Body of Christ!

CHAPTER 14

From the Podium of Fear to the Platform of Freedom

Religion vs. Freedom: Nervous Breakdowns vs. Divine Authority

If you mentioned public speaking, I was going to run for my life. I feared it like nothing else—not only because of the trembling in my voice I couldn't hide , but because of the *movement* in my stomach that would show up whenever I began to speak. It would make my voice drop almost to a whisper, like I was being muzzled. I was ashamed of it and dared not tell a soul that something was stirring inside me. It remained my little secret until my prophetic trainer instructed me to seek the Lord about doubt. During one of our class sessions, she said to me, *"Tiffany, I want you to sit with the Lord and ask Him what the root of your doubt is, because I see it all over you."* My question to the Holy Spirit was, *Did someone say something to me as a child that I don't remember—something that makes me doubt myself?*

The Holy Spirit immediately took me back to my childhood

and drew my attention to one of my older cousins. Then He replayed moments where I watched her and felt sorry for her, because she struggled with what the adults called a "nervous condition." It was so bad that one day, all of us kids were making our usual ruckus in the van. When we got back to my aunt's house, my uncle swung the door open—and out tumbled my cousin, We all got in trouble, but I felt so bad for her. I can still remember saying to myself, *I hope I don't be like her... but I feel like I already am.*

As those memories began to fade, I asked, "Lord, is that it?" My pastor was in the prophetic class with us, so she heard the instruction given to me. After I sought the Lord, I shared with her what I believed He had revealed as the root of my doubt, and she said she would seek Him in prayer. The Lord confirmed to my pastor that this was indeed where the door to doubt had been opened—when I empathized with my cousin, that door had opened. My pastor and I scheduled a deliverance session to call out the **spirit of Leviathan**, and unbeknownst to me, that was the day I would be delivered from the "monster" in my stomach I had never told a soul about. At the end of the session, my pastor asked me how I felt. I replied, "I feel fine." She smiled and said, "Okay, well, I'm about to test it. We're doing *Obedience October,* and you're one of the live speakers. How do you feel?"

I stood for a moment to see if that nervousness, fear, or doubt would rise up—because I didn't have to wait for it to show up at the event; most times, it came as soon as someone said I'd be speaking in front of a crowd. That day, nothing showed up. I laughed, thanked God, and accepted the assignment. And guess what? The assignment was completed.

I won't lie and say fear didn't show up—the enemy was on

his job. However, my job was to push past fear and do it anyway! *"For God has not given us a spirit of fear, but of power and of love and of a sound mind."* II Timothy 1:7, (NKJV)

As I continue to walk this journey, I decree that I accept every assignment to speak with divine authority, because nervousness, doubt, and fear are not my portion.

Then vs. Now:
Photos, Memories, and the Testimony of Transformation

I am a witness that God is a healer and a good, good Father. Deliverance is for the **decided**, and there is work that comes with it. This has not been easy—but it's been worth it. You know the saying, *"Anything worth having is worth fighting for."* Don't be afraid of the fight—you're already fighting, just often the wrong thing.

It is only because of Him that today I can stand tall, because I am seated in heavenly places with Him (Ephesians 2:6). I now respond instead of react. I allow myself to feel what I feel, knowing God doesn't require me to rush past the emotions He gave me.

> *I choose to remain single until He sends the one He has chosen for me.*
> *I choose to follow the freedom of Christ and be led by the Spirit—not my flesh.*
> *I choose to love myself above everyone else.*
> *I choose to live an abundant life.*
> *I choose to be His living sacrifice.*
> *I choose to accept the cost of the oil.*
> *I choose to walk in the fruit of the Spirit—to be loving,*

joyful, peaceful, patient, kind, good, faithful, gentle, and operate in self-control (Galatians 5:22–23). I choose to look, act, walk, and talk like my Father, because I am indeed an #AbbasGirl—choosing all these things freely by choice, not by the force of rule-keeping.

From Afraid to Called, From Silenced to Sent

IN BONDAGE THE FREEDOM FRAME

There's no turning back. *Here comes extra!* That's what my Father told me one day when I said to Him, "I don't want people to think I'm extra." His reply was, *"BE EXTRA."* And He even gave me a scripture to support it:

> *"With all this going for us, my dear, dear friends, stand your ground. And don't hold back. Throw yourselves into the work of the Master, confident that nothing you do for Him is a waste of time or effort." I Corinthians 15:58, (MSG)*

Everything I've endured throughout my life has prepared me for such a time as this. I may not understand all He has done and will do—but I don't need to understand to obey Him. He never commanded us to understand Him; He told us to trust Him and *lean not to our own understanding* (Proverbs 3:5–6).

As Jehovah Gibbor, the Mighty Warrior who defends and protects me.

As Jehovah Shalom, my peace in the midst of the storm. And as Jehovah Rapha, the undefeated Healer.

In the 'Bondage' photo, I was asked to read the Word *(bible)* for that service and I was terrified. I didn't like going up in front of crowds, period. It didn't matter if I had a script, text or not. It was a NO and it showed on my face. The lack of confidence!!

The Freedom Frame photo, while I had a goofy look on my face, I was very confident in Christ. I was nervous, but I wasn't bound. I was asked to be one of the speakers for the '7 Last Words' service. I freely spoke, I didn't overthink it, I laughed at myself and I showed up as me and sometimes I am goofy!

One thing this journey has done is increase my trust and faith in Him. I know Him as Jehovah Shammah, the One who is always there. He has my best interests at heart and knows all the plans He has for my life (Jeremiah 29:11). He doesn't waste a thing, and all things have worked together for my good (Romans 8:28).

- I am no longer afraid of my Father because I've been called by my Father.

- I am no longer afraid of people's opinions because what they think about me is none of my business.
- I didn't go through the fire to be the same—or to be silent.

So, ready or not…
Here we come.

AFTERWORD

— BY SHAY JOHNSON —

Have you ever felt trapped in a cloud of negativity—as if something unseen has been holding you back and wondered if there's more to life than what you've been experiencing? That the people around you seem to be living in an unbreakable cycle, while you've been on a spiritual rollercoaster for far too long? You feel drained and depleted, yet you can't quite explain why.

What if I told you that Tiffany Melvin has received a spiritual download—a divine gateway that many fear to enter but one that leads to true freedom? You've heard the saying, "Anything worth having is worth fighting for" — and nothing is more worth fighting for than your freedom.

There is a spiritual war raging against your soul, and without realizing it, you may have unknowingly entered into word agreements that gave the enemy legal access to your life. The journey toward complete healing and freedom can make you weary, but there is hope. By the leading of the Holy Spirit, today marks a new beginning. It's time to come out of your grave clothes and walk in your newness.

Breaking the Good Girl Syndrome is not just a manual — it's a blueprint from God designed to shift your perspective and help you see your life clearly again. It awakens you to the freedom God intended for you from the foundation of the world.

I've known Tiffany Melvin for years, and I have seen her battle scars. I can tell you firsthand: her heart's desire is for you to live your best life — free, healed, and whole, resting in Christ's redemptive love.

> I challenge you today; pause and examine yourself.
> Where are you stuck—in your mind, body, or soul?

We all carry wounds, whether from childhood trauma, betrayal, rejection, or painful experiences with people we once trusted. Some of these wounds have held us in bondage for years, causing us to lose ourselves while trying to fit into places we were never meant to belong. The Word reminds us in *Galatians 5:1, NIV "It is for freedom that Christ has set us free. Stand firm, then, and do not let yourselves be burdened again by a yoke of slavery."*

In this transformational work, Tiffany uses her life's journey as a roadmap, exposing the hidden walls and strongholds that prevent us from experiencing the fullness of God's divine plan.

You'll discover how the wounds of legalism can silently destroy the soul if left unattended and unhealed. How the masks of religion we often wear to hide our pain, fearing judgment and rejection, can become a silent killer—both naturally and spiritually.

How embracing vulnerability and God's unconditional love empowers you to override the snares of the enemy and step into true freedom. This journey requires bravery, but you are not alone. Tiffany has walked through her darkest valleys and discovered the light at the end of the tunnel—and I have walked that journey, too.

I know what it means for God to heal deep, rooted childhood wounds.
I grew up under constant attack from my mother, who battled schizophrenia and bipolar disorder. I struggled with abandonment and rejection from my father.

In 1993, I joined a ministry that taught me a performance-based faith, which caused me to develop a judgmental heart. I survived a near-death drowning experience, being kidnapped and raped multiple times, and yet, God never left me. He still loved me!

My true transformation began at my "woman at the well" moment with Jesus. In His presence, He unveiled the depths of my heart, spoke life into my brokenness, and offered me His living water. I accepted it, and from that moment on, I was never the same.

Breaking the Good Girl Syndrome is more than a book— it's a spiritual encounter. It's a study guide designed to help you take notes, dig deeper, and walk boldly into healing and deliverance. It's an invitation to drink from the living water Jesus offers, to break every chain, and to step into the abundant life God has promised you.

This is your moment.
This is your freedom.
This is your awakening.

— Apostle Shay Johnson
Sweet Aroma Divine Ministries
Raleigh, NC

ACKNOWLEDGEMENTS

Glory and honor to my **Abba Father**, who came for me. Without You, there would be no *Breaking the Good Girl Syndrome*—because I would still be bound by religion. Thank You for loving me so much that You caused a divine interruption in my life just to give me freedom.

Jesus, I've known Your hand for a very long time, but it is through freedom that I found Your face. I love and adore You so much! Your Daughter, *Tiffany* #TheVeryManifestationofGod

To my beautiful daughter and Woman of High Faith, Jamesha Abri' Ruffin,

When I was at my lowest point in life, you invited me to take family photos with you and the kids to lift my spirits. Hands down, you have the biggest heart — full of thoughtfulness and love. You will never know how much that meant to me and how clearly I saw your heart in that moment. Thank you for your love and for your prayers for my healing. I love you dearly, my sweet Mini-Me!

To my handsome son and Quiet Thunder, Kyleaf Taisod Cameron-Battle,

I am so proud of the man you are becoming. Thank you for holding things down financially during the onset of the WWF Smackdown of 2018. As a teenager, you were forced into a role that no one prepared you for, and you took on a household head-on without complaint. I am forever grateful for your considerate and big heart. I love you dearly, my Big Baby! Oh, and thank you for #Luffy!!

To my grandbabies, Jayda, Sarai, Ollie (Olivia), and Jayce,

The four of you mean the world to me — and don't you ever forget that. I am so proud to be your grandmother. When I look at your faces, I truly feel *joy* in my heart. As you grow, I want to remind you to always keep God first, build a relationship with Him, and honor Him with your life. I love you all so much!

To my mother, Selema Johnson,

Without you, there is no me. Thank you for the many sacrifices you made for me as a child. Thank you for the love that continues to *scream out loud* for me, and thank you for always being present in my life and never turning your back on me. You are indeed my number one girl! I love you so much, Mama — and don't ever forget that, okay?

To my Pop, Zander Johnson,
We've experienced many things together, but there is one moment that truly solidified your love for me — when you took the time to pray with and for me every Wednesday for three months straight. They say people who pray for you love you, so thank you for loving me and for being one of my biggest cheerleaders, always telling me how brilliant I am. I AGREE, lol.

Can you believe it? I WROTE A BOOK — I'm a whole AUTHOR, Pop!! Thank you for always believing in me and for reminding me that I am indeed your favorite Tiffany. I love you dearly.

To my best friend and sister, Lenita Henderson, whom I've known since the age of 15.

You are the only person who has experienced so many versions of me, and there is one thing that remains true — your friendship has been a faithful one through the good, the bad, and the ugly. Thank you for your listening ear, prayers, and wise counsel. Thank you for enduring all my ugly cries throughout my freedom journey and for always reminding me it's "Team Tiffany," no matter what! I love you so much!!

To my sistacuzzin, friend, and wise counselor, Donna Brodie Kidd,

This relationship has been forged through the fire for sure. Thank you for always being a source of wisdom in my life. I can remember asking you years ago, "How do you know when you have forgiven someone?" and you posed a question back to me: "How do you feel when you think of the person?" You followed that with, "If you feel anything other than love, you have not forgiven them." Your response then and now has remained the same — full of sound, biblical advice, always encouraging me to search my heart until nothing was there. Guess what? Nothing is there — I have forgiven! ~ I love you dearly!

To my sister and writing accountability partner, Minister Tifany Ross,

GIRLLLLL — words can't even express how much I appreciate your push. Thank you for all the writing sessions that kept me on track. Thank you for your prayers and your love. I love you!

To all of my spiritual leaders I met along the way on this journey of Freedom:

To Pastor Rose Thomas,

Back in 2018, at the beginning of my spiritual transition, there was a period when the only instruction I had from God was to simply "LEAVE" the church I was attending. I had no clue where I was going. I was afraid, broken, and in so much agony when I came to your church to visit. You welcomed me with such love, peace, and care as I attended your teaching on "Soul Ties"—so indicative of the Father! Thank you so much for being the first to initiate loving me back to life. I love you dearly!

To Overseer Kysha Jones Thompson,

Thank you for answering the call to tear down religion! Your *YES* meant my freedom, and I am so thankful to have experienced your leadership. I am proud to be your *fruit*, and I pray God's strength over you as you continue to lead so many of His people out of bondage into freedom. I honor you, and I love you very much.

To Pastor Ebony Freeland Bryant,

Last but certainly not least! Thank you for your pouring, your love, and your cheerleader spirit. I have never had a leader make me feel as capable as you, and I am thankful for all the growth I've experienced because of your leadership. Thank you for the countless laughter, the working out with me, and the encouragement to just be me. I love you!

ABOUT THE AUTHOR

Ms. Tiffany Sherell Melvin was born on September 9, 1971, in Durham, North Carolina, to the late Charles "Jerry" Cameron and Ms. Selema Mae Alston. Tiffany cherishes her roles as a devoted mother to two adult children, Jamesha Ruffin and Kyleaf Cameron-Battle, and as a proud grandmother to four beautiful grandchildren: Jayda, Sarai, Olivia, and Jayce.

She is the owner of Creative Council Studios, home of the Freedom Frame Photography experience, where faith and artistry unite to tell redemptive stories of identity, confidence, and divine purpose. Tiffany also leads Scores Up Financial Services, LLC, and is a Certified Peer Support Specialist in Mental Health, extending compassion and practical wisdom to those navigating personal restoration and growth.

A creative at heart, Tiffany holds an Associate Degree in Business Administration and has pursued collegiate studies in Fashion, Style, and Merchandise, merging business acumen with an eye for beauty and excellence. Of all the titles she carries, serving as a **Prophetic** Intercessor is her greatest joy; a sacred calling endeavor she pursues.

Beyond her professional achievements, Tiffany delights in life's simple joys. She loves films such as Gladiator, Troy, and Bad Boys, and has a soft spot for actor Adam Sandler. Her soul finds peace by the ocean, where laughter, prayer, and dance often meet.

Tiffany's faith is her compass. She believes that every gift bestowed upon her carries both purpose and responsibility. With unwavering devotion, her mission remains steadfast: to channel her creativity, compassion, and courage for the greater glory of God, and to leave an indelible mark on every life divinely connected to hers.

CALL to ACTION

Let's Continue the Journey Together

Freedom isn't a one-time moment—it's a lifestyle of becoming who God designed you to be. If *Breaking the Good Girl Syndrome* spoke to your heart, there's more waiting for you.

→ Dive Deeper into the Message

Join Tiffany for exclusive reflections, resources, and Freedom Frame™ experiences that help you walk out your healing and identity in everyday life.

✨ Subscribe for updates, events, and Freedom Frame™
sessions at:

👉 www.CreativeCouncilStudios.com/freedom-frame

→ Invite Tiffany to Speak

Tiffany is available for:

- Women's conferences and retreats
- Faith-based leadership gatherings
- Healing and identity workshops
- Creative and entrepreneurial events

Through transparent storytelling, prophetic insight, and authentic connection, Tiffany helps audiences rediscover their worth, release perfectionism, and embrace divine purpose.

To book Tiffany:
Email: **creativecouncilme@gmail.com**
Subject Line: *Speaking Opportunity for Tiffany Melvin*

Include event date, location, and topic or theme. Tiffany's team will respond promptly with speaking details and availability.

→ **Experience The Freedom Frame™**

Step into a photography encounter that's more than a photoshoot—it's a prophetic, faith-centered moment of healing, identity, and joy.

The *Freedom Frame*™ *Experience* combines artistry and spiritual reflection to visually capture your transformation. Each session is designed to help women see themselves through God's eyes—not their mistakes or pain, but their divine identity and freedom.

→ **Book your session:**
www.CreativeCouncilStudios.com/freedom-frame
or **creativecouncilme@gmail.com**

→ **Partner, Collaborate, or Connect**

Tiffany also welcomes creative partnerships for:

- Collaborative Freedom Frame™ pop-ups at women's events
- Book + Photography bundles for conferences
- Panel or podcast interviews on identity and healing

To collaborate, reach out via:
Email: **creativecouncilme@gmail.com**

"You were never called to be perfect—you were called to be free. Don't just read the message. *Live it*!
Step into your freedom, on purpose."

— **Tiffany Sherrell Melvin**
Founder, *Creative Council Studios*
Author, *Breaking the Good Girl Syndrome*

BOOK REVIEW

"**Breaking the Good Girl Syndrome**" is a powerful and transparent journey that speaks directly to the heart of anyone who has ever felt bound by the chains of religious legalism and the resulting cycles of guilt and shame. The author's honesty in sharing her struggles makes this book both relatable and liberating.

It is medicine for the soul—healing truth delivered with a sweet hint of humor. Tiffany reveals, with grace and boldness, how God's love dismantles performance-based faith and invites us into true intimacy with Him.

This book beautifully affirms our God-given identity and calls us to walk in freedom rather than fear. It is more than a testimony—it's a roadmap to healing, restoration, and an authentic covenant relationship with God.

– Lenita Henderson
Program Manager
North Carolina

BOOK REVIEW

All I can say is, *"Chiiillle!"* Real, raw, and uncut! Tiffany shares her story with unapologetic honesty and unmatched authenticity. I've witnessed her transformation firsthand—the moment she resolutely proclaimed, *"Enough!"*

Breaking the Good Girl Syndrome offers an intimate glimpse into the challenges my good sis faced and ultimately conquered. She details the struggles and triumphs, walking you through every symptom associated with the Good Girl Syndrome, and proves that it can indeed be overcome.

Deliverance is for the decided—and Tiffany's decision and obedience have positioned her to lead others into the same promise of **FREEDOM** that awaits those who choose to break free.

– Min. Shunte' M. Bryant
Founder, Divine Connections NC
Owner & Doula, 4YOU Doula Services

BOOK REVIEW

Reading "Breaking the Good Girl Syndrome" was like holding up a mirror. Tiffany is my first cousin, so much of her story—her struggles, her healing—felt deeply familiar to me. Yet even with that familiarity, her words pulled me in with such force that I found myself reliving moments, feeling the weight of the fears she described, and celebrating the freedom she now walks in.

This book ignited a compassion in me that I didn't expect. It stirred a *holy anger* toward how religion can wound, and a profound joy in witnessing the power of God's love to heal.

Tiffany writes with raw honesty and prophetic authority. Her testimony is a declaration that freedom is not only possible—it is promised. I didn't just read her story; I *felt* it, I *celebrated* it, and I walked away with renewed faith that God still delivers.

– Donna Brodie Kidd
Founder, Donna Kidd Ministries
Advocates for the Inner Wounded, Inc.
Visionary of the *"I'm Coming for the Little Girl" (Inner Healing)*
Movement

Evangelist · Prophetic Intercessor · Deliverance Minister · Psalmist

www.ingramcontent.com/pod-product-compliance
Lightning Source LLC
Chambersburg PA
CBHW050112170426
43198CB00014B/2547